GOLF

LEGENDS
PLAYERS · HOLES
LIFE ON THE TOURS

Angus G. Garber III

GALLERY BOOKS
An Imprint of W. H. Smith Publishers Inc.
New York, New York 10016

A FRIEDMAN GROUP BOOK

Published by GALLERY BOOKS
An imprint of W.H. Smith Publishers, Inc.
112 Madison Avenue
New York, New York 10016

ISBN 0-8317-3923-1

GOLF LEGENDS: Players...Holes...Life on the Tours
was prepared and produced by
Michael Friedman Publishing Group, Inc.
15 West 26th Street
New York, New York 10010

Editor: Bruce Lubin
Art Director: Mary Moriarty
Designer: Robert W. Kosturko
Photo Editor: Christopher Bain
Production Manager: Karen L. Greenberg

Typeset by Best-set Typesetter Ltd.
Color separations by South Sea International Press Ltd.
Printed and bound in Hong Kong by Leefung-Asco Printers Ltd.

Santa Fe Island is home to a healthy population of Galápagos hawks that enjoy a protected habitat amidst Opuntia cactus.

INDEX

Dedication

For Angus G. Garber I, who put the first club in my hands.

Acknowledgements

Many thanks to those who shared their understanding of this elegant game: Bruce "Bruiser" Berlet, the talented golf writer for the Hartford Courant; the good people who provide information on the PGA, LPGA, and Seniors Tours; Hank Gola and John Delery, whose passion for the game is exceeded only by their inability to master it; editor Bruce Lubin of the Michael Friedman Publishing Group; my wife, Gerry, whose capacity for patience is unending and amazing.

C O N T

E N T S

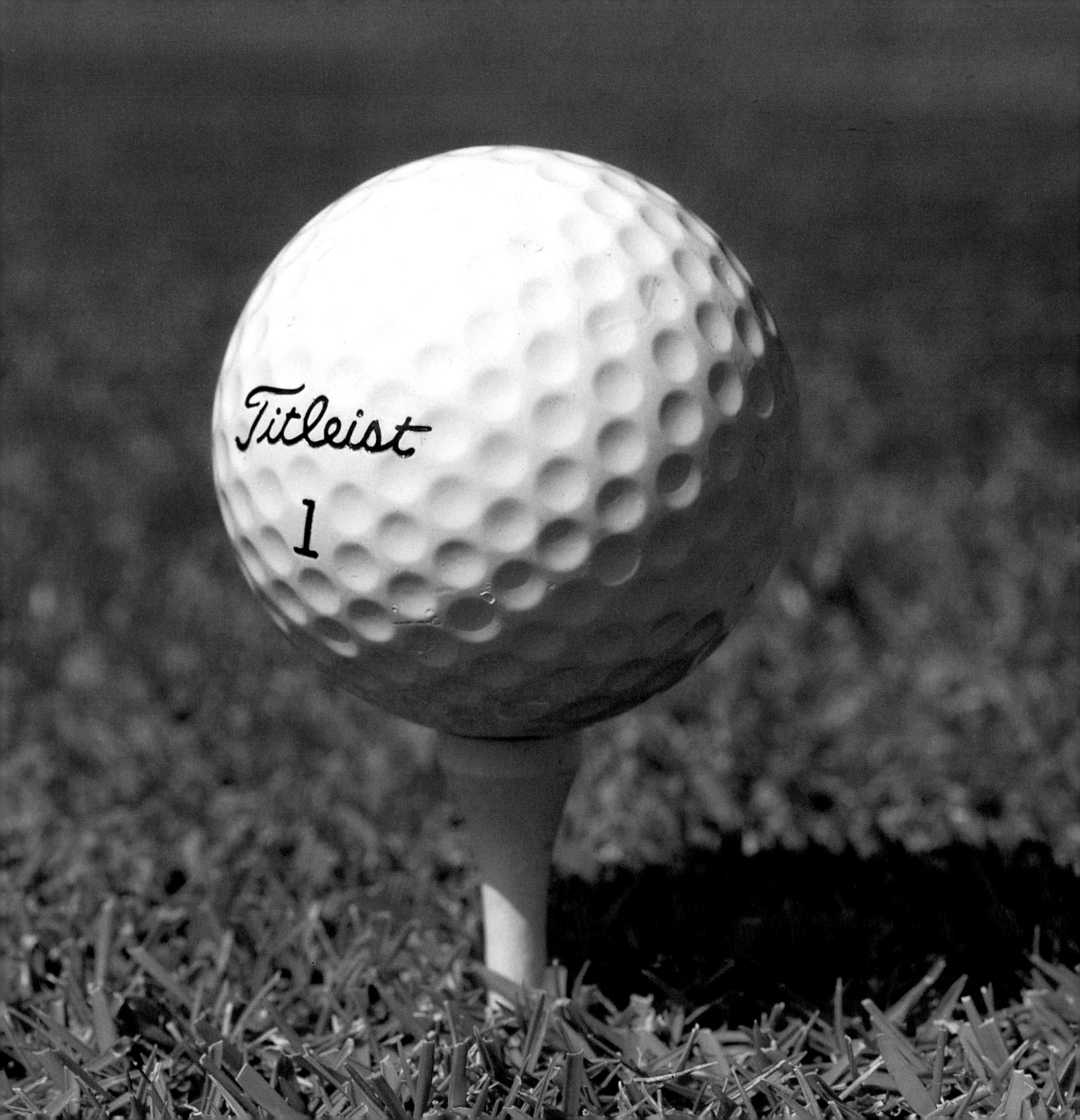
Titleist
1

Introduction

THE GAME OF GOLF IS NOT MERELY A STRUGGLE OF man against nature. It pits man against an even more formidable adversary: Himself. And this horrible, exhilarating, internal, and eternal tug-of-war is what makes the game so loved — and hated.

Simply put, golf is different from other sports. This isn't tennis, where even a good shot can be erased with a better one by an opponent. Unlike basketball, no one can steal the ball as you prepare to address it properly. In baseball, the pitcher tries to deceive the hitter into offering at a curveball in the dirt; football introduces violence and physical persuasion into the equation. Yes, golf is marvelously different: When you hit the ball, no one hits it back. The golfer, and the golfer alone, is responsible for where the ball comes to rest. And thus time magnifies the shot, good or bad. A crisp three-iron that drops the ball fifteen feet from the hole in birdie range can send the

golfer's ego running rampant as he strides up the fairway. It can also propel the ball six feet past the cup on the next shot, leaving bogey a distinct possibility. Similarly, the slice into the rough off the tee can leave a man doubting himself. When the subsequent three-iron to the green lands short, in a monstrous sand trap, confidence and the chance for a good eighteen-hole score can be shattered.

These vagaries of the game have made heroes of Arnold Palmer and Jack Nicklaus. And every once in a while golf brings even heroes to their knees. "You're never ahead for long," Nicklaus says. "Sooner or later, the course is going to get you."

Who is to blame for this maddening sport? The Scottish like to think they invented the game, but there is evidence that, like many good ideas, golf evolved slowly through time. In fact, man has been hitting balls with sticks, or hitting stones with tree limbs, since he began walking the

© Fred Roe

Although golf has been played throughout the ages, its popularity rocketed in the 1960s thanks to Arnold Palmer, who attracted legions of fans (left). Prior to Palmer's arrival, Ben Hogan (right) had been golf's dominant force.

earth in an upright position — it's just that there wasn't an assistant pro standing behind him murmuring something about keeping his head down and swinging through the ball. It is quite possible the Dutch were the first to formalize the game, sometime during the sixteenth century. Of course, since frozen canals dominated the landscape, the Dutch rolled in their eight-foot putts for par on ice.

At the same time, the Scots were making refinements of their own. In fact, golf grew so popular in the 1400s that King James II abolished it because the game was interfering with archery practice — and in the 1400s, archery was a major form of national defense. In theory, this probably was sound judgment, but history suggests the general public nevertheless kept hacking away. In 1502, King James IV was observed playing golf and the floodgates opened once again. Organized groups existed

for more than a hundred years, but it wasn't until 1744 that the Honourable Company of Edinburgh Golfers was formed. "Several Gentlemen of Honour, Skillful in the ancient and healthfull exercise of Golf," as the Edinburgh charter read, persuaded the magistrates of Edinburgh to provide a silver cup for their annual competitions. All comers were welcome, and rules were drawn up to avoid controversy. The first effort was a complete disaster. The winner was John Rattray, a local surgeon, in a field of twelve.

In 1860, the first British Open was held at Prestwick links in Scotland. Eight professional entrants toured the twelve-hole course three times, and Willie Park emerged as the winner, shooting a blazing 174. William Steel, who wasn't as good as his name, took 232, including a single-hole total of twenty-one. After twelve years at Prestwick, the British Open moved to St. Andrews and subsequently

© Fred Roe

rotated every year among an expanding roster of dignified courses. Over the years, the game gradually gained consistency and momentum.

In America, they played the first U.S. Open in 1895, at Newport Golf Club in Rhode Island. Horace Rawlins was the winner with a thirty-six-hole total of 173. It wasn't until 1913, when British heavyweight Harry Vardon made his second visit to America, that golf first became widely recognized. Vardon had already won three British Opens and the 1900 U.S. Open at Chicago Golf Club, and this time he brought with him Ted Ray, the reigning British Open champion. A twenty-year-old amateur from Boston named Francis Ouimet beat them in a playoff for the title, and golf was never quite the same in the colonies. The Masters was born in Augusta, Georgia, in 1934, and in the 1950s President Dwight D. Eisenhower took delight in chasing the dimpled white ball. Twenty years later,

President Gerald Ford, a former football player, gained notoriety for his errant drives. He took pleasure in noting that most of his bad shots were slices, hit with a Republican sensibility — to the right.

Today, golf is big business. Great Britain, Japan, West Germany, and Australia are only a few of the places it thrives. America supports three tours: The Professional Golfers Association, the Ladies Professional Golfer's Association, and the Seniors Tour. In 1987, they collectively offered approximately $50 million in prizes. There are golf courses, driving ranges, and miniature-golf facilities all over the world. Golf offers a sense of egalitarianism that is impossible to argue with: For each action, there is an equal and opposite reaction. You have no one to blame but yourself. And so this splendor in the grass appeals to people of all ages and backgrounds.

If King James II had only known.

The Players

TOM MORRIS, SR., WON THE SECOND BRITISH OPEN IN 1861, THEN repeated his feat the following year, again edging Willie Park on the Prestwick, Scotland, links. Old Tom Morris won the title again in 1864 and 1867. Then the title was wrested away by a younger man — Tom Morris, Jr., the game's first truly great player.

Young Tom, as he was called for obvious reasons, was seventeen years and five months old when he won his first British Open championship. Old Tom was second. His son won the title three years in a row and then retired the championship belt and the generous six-pound prize that went with it. As a result, the British Open was not played in 1871 — when the British retire something, after all, they retire it. Young Tom came back to win in 1872, completing an unequaled sweep of four consecutive championships. Young Tom died at the age of twenty-four, but he is remembered as one of golf's greatest legends.

Like Young Tom Morris, some learned the game from their parents. Greg Norman, one of the world's best players, learned golf from his mother. Others like Sam Snead and Seve Ballesteros discovered the game on their own, fashioning clubs out of the crudest materials. All of them are athletes, despite what the rest of the sporting establishment would have you believe. Babe Didrikson Zaharias, for instance, was a world-class sprinter before she took up golf.

They come in different sizes — at 6-foot-1, 190 pounds, Norman dwarfs the 5-foot-7, 150-pound Gary Player — and shapes (no one would ever confuse a profile of burly Jack Nicklaus and the rail-thin Ben Hogan), but their common denominator is competitive fire. All the great ones had it, from Ballesteros to Harry Vardon. The women, from Mickey Wright to JoAnne Carner to Nancy Lopez, also shared the same indomitable spirit.

Here are their stories.

A meeting of the legends: Tom Watson and Sam Snead share a story while out on the course.

Seve Ballesteros has always played with a confident air, but since 1984 he has run into problems with the PGA Tour. A rule stipulating that members of a foreign tour must compete in fifteen events a year in the U.S.A. to gain full Tour status left Ballesteros—one of the globe's busiest golfers—a persona non grata.

Severiano Ballesteros

MOST OF THOSE WHO ALLOW EMOTIONS TO RULE THEIR golf game are very quickly left behind, to languish over an unending series of six-foot comeback putts for par in golfing purgatory. Not so Severiano Ballesteros.

In a game heavily populated by placid, prototypical blonds, Ballesteros is a dark, forbidding alternative. He plays his slashing, go-for-broke game with a formidable heart on his sweater sleeve. Seve Ballesteros is nothing if not exciting. Historically, this has worked both for and against him. The successes, however, have far outweighed the failures and this remains Ballesteros' peculiar place in golf: There have been fleeting times when he has defeated the game itself on his own daring terms.

He was born in Pedrena, Spain, and first fashioned clubs from sticks he found along the Bay of Santander. Ballesteros would force the stick into the head of a three-iron discarded by his older brothers and soak it in a pail of water overnight. By morning, the makeshift effort had become, very temporarily, a golf club. There were no proper golf balls, of course, and Ballesteros would seek out the roundest, finest stones and blast away at them for as long as his club would last.

It was in those overgrown fields in Spain that Ballesteros learned the game of golf, as well as the value of resourcefulness. To this day, Ballesteros can create new shots every time he tees the ball up. He is one of the most gifted iron players in history, often able to extricate himself from the deepest holes his drives leave him in.

In 1976, Ballesteros was a nineteen-year-old professional who for three years had already played golf in all four corners of the world. For three rounds, Ballesteros held off Johnny Miller at Royal Birkdale with the British Open on the line. Miller eventually won, but Ballesteros finished tied for second with Jack Nicklaus.

© Jim Moriarty

From 1976 to 1978, Ballesteros was Europe's leading money-winner, amassing titles in Australia, Ireland, Holland, Kenya, and Switzerland, among others.

Ballesteros took home the British Open championship in 1979, edging Ben Crenshaw and Nicklaus at Royal Lytham. He became the first Continental player to win the oldest title since Arnaud Massy did it in 1907. A year later, Ballesteros made history again, by becoming the first European and only the second non-American to win the Masters at Augusta National. (South Africa's Gary Player had won in 1961.) Ballesteros added another green jacket in 1983.

In 1984, Ballesteros beat a truly international field at St. Andrews in Scotland, holding off Tom Watson and West Germany's Bernhard Langer for his second British Open title. Four major titles in six years established Ballesteros as a truly global golfing talent.

Ballesteros has the rare ability to consistently excite golf galleries. By the age of twenty-seven, he had won two Masters championships, along with two British Open titles. In the fall of 1987, Ballesteros led the European team to victory over the United States (above) in a dramatic Ryder Cup competition.

JOANNE CARNER, A LARGER-THAN-LIFE PRESENCE ON THE LPGA tour, has had two careers that have distinguished her as one of the greatest to ever play the game.

The first was as an amateur, when she exerted more force on the women's circuit than anyone since Babe Zaharias. Carner was born in Kirkland, Washington, on April 4, 1939, and seventeen years later won the 1956 Girl's Junior Championship. In 1957, at age eighteen, she won her first U.S. Amateur Championship; this was followed by victories in 1960, 1962, 1966, and 1968, for a still-standing record of five wins. You have to go back to Beatrice Hoyt in 1896 to find a titlist so young. Carner was a competitor on four different Curtis Cup teams, and she remains the last amateur to win an LPGA event, the 1969 Burdine's Invitational in Miami. That experience left her rethinking her future, and in 1970 there was suddenly a thirty-year-old rookie loose on the ladies' tour.

The professional Carner was every bit as successful. Her first money came at the Burdine's Invitational, where she earned $305 for placing in a tie for thirty-sixth. Carner won the Wendell West Open in her first season on the LPGA tour and, ultimately, the Rookie of the Year. She won the U.S. Open in 1971 and placed sixth overall on the tour before a two-year drought that saw her finish fifteenth and twenty-sixth, respectively. And then JoAnne Carner, a 5-foot-7 competitor who came to be known as Big Momma for her muscular approach to the game, started to dominate golf all over again.

She won $87,094 in 1974 to lead all women golfers in earnings; for the next eleven years, Carner would rank among

USGA Golf House

JoAnne Carner

JoAnne Carner was known as "the Great Gundy"—her maiden name was Gunderson—when she put together one of the greatest amateur records in the history of the sport. In 1969, Carner beat a field of professionals in the Burdine's Invitational. After passing up the winner's check of a few thousand dollars, Carner decided to turn professional a year later.

the top ten. She took six titles that year, a personal high. There were three more championships in 1975 and $64,843 in winnings, good for second place. Another U.S. Open title came in 1976, and Carner cleared $100,000 for the first time. She would duplicate the feat eight times in the next nine years. On August 30, 1981, Carner won the Columbia Savings tournament and collected $22,000 — that gave her more than a million in winnings, leaving her as the second woman to reach that plateau. (Kathy Whitworth had became the first only a month earlier with a third place at the U.S. Open.)

That year Carner began a three-season run as golf's dominant female player. In 1981, she was second in winnings and followed with two first-place finishes. Over that stretch, Carner won eleven tournaments and $808,451. Fittingly, the United States Golf Association made her only the fifth woman to receive the Bob Jones Award for sportsmanship in 1981. Carner, who was the first LPGA athlete to ring up three consecutive years of more than $200,000 in earnings, became the second woman golfer to reach the $2 million mark.

Through 1986, Carner won forty-two tournaments, $2,013,992, three Player of the Year honors, and five Vare Trophies for lowest stroke average. In 1982, Carner was enshrined in the LPGA Hall of Fame.

Though back pain has limited her effectiveness in recent years, Carner is still a fixture on the LPGA tour. She travels the circuit in a motor home with her husband, Don, or relaxes with a fishing pole in her hands on the Tellico River in Tennessee.

The tenth woman to be inducted into the World Golf Hall of Fame (in 1985), Carner credits Gordon Jenkins, John Hoetmer, Gardner Dickinson, and Sam Snead for influencing her career. In thirteen of her seventeen seasons as a professional, Carner managed at least one first-place finish, a testimony to her enduring talent.

TO WIN 51 PROFESSIONAL GOLFERS' ASSOCIATION EVENTS is a major achievement. Only six men have ever done it (and five of them are named Sam Snead, Jack Nicklaus, Ben Hogan, Arnold Palmer, and Byron Nelson). To win fifty-one titles and remain anything less than a living legend is a feat for the history books. Such is the underrated nature of Billy Casper's fine career in golfing.

He didn't blast the ball off the tee in the manner of Jack Nicklaus, or strike particularly splendid long irons to the green. His putter was serviceable, but not a deadly weapon in his

Billy Casper

© R. Mackson/FPG Intl.

gentle hands. Overall, Casper's sweet seven-iron was his best club, which says a lot about the man. Casper's game was well rounded and consistent, unspectacular yet relentlessly effective.

Casper was born on June 24, 1931, in San Diego, California, and attended the University of Notre Dame. During college he was discovered by some San Diego businessmen and immediately staked to a year on the PGA Tour. Casper, a stout 5-foot-11, 215 pounds, almost immediately repaid their faith.

He won the Labatt Open in 1956 and would continue to win at least one title for each of the next fifteen years. Only Nicklaus and Palmer (seventeen consecutive years) won over a longer period of time. Casper won the U.S. Open at Winged Foot Golf Club in Mamaroneck, New York, in 1959, edging Bob Rosburg. That was also the first of three consecutive years Casper would triumph in the Portland Open — an accomplishment only Walter Hagen's four straight PGA championships surpassed.

By 1965, Casper's weight, always a problem, had become something of a nightmare. Finally, a Chicago doctor discovered that he was allergic to a number of common foods. Thus alerted, Casper went on to play the best golf of his career. His U.S. Open victory in 1966 is considered a classic.

Given Casper's countenance, that incredible victory at Olympic Country Club in San Francisco is remembered more for Arnold Palmer's collapse than Casper's win. The two players had been tied after thirty-six holes, but Palmer made his move on the third day and stretched his lead to seven shots with nine holes left to play on Sunday. Impossibly, Casper caught him. As Palmer slowly became unraveled, Casper quietly made birdie after birdie. He shot a 32 on the back nine, which, coupled with Palmer's 39, gave both men a 278-stroke total. On Monday, the eighteen-hole playoff unfolded in similar fashion. Palmer held a two-stroke lead after nine holes, then Casper worked his way back. He dropped a 50-foot birdie putt on No. 13 on his way to a 69. Palmer shot 73, and though he had won eight major tournaments in his dazzling career, would never win another. The next year, Palmer finished second to Nicklaus at Baltusrol Golf Club in New Jersey. Casper was the PGA's Player of the Year in 1966 and won one of his five Vardon Trophies then.

Casper, ever the money player, won the 1970 Masters in another playoff, this time defeating Gene Littler. Earlier that year,

Casper's victory in the Los Angeles Open made him only the second player in history to reach the million-dollar mark in earnings. When Casper left the PGA Tour in 1981 to join the Senior Tour, he had won those fifty-one tournaments and $1,686,458. Through 1986, the numbers had risen to fifty-six and $2,369,078.

In 1983, Casper displayed his playoff grit again. He and Rod Funseth finished the United States Senior Open at even-par 288, but Casper won in the 18-hole playoff. Spectacular? Perhaps not, but Billy Casper always knew how to win.

He didn't have the charisma of Arnie or Jack, but Billy Casper (right) knew how to win golf tournaments. From the 1956 Labatt's title to a triumph at the New Orleans Open in 1975, Casper won fifty-one championships in his years on the PGA Tour. His most celebrated win was the 1966 triumph over Arnold Palmer in the U.S. Open, when Casper rallied from seven strokes down with nine holes to play on the final day. In 1983 (left) he took the USGA Senior Open in an 18-hole playoff with Rod Funseth at Hazeltine Golf Club. Friends say Casper has mellowed with age, as his fashion indicates.

USGA Golf House

Babe Didrikson Zaharias was an athlete, pure and simple. In a poll conducted by the Associated Press, she was named Woman Athlete of the First Half of the 20th Century. She could do virtually anything in athletics, yet chose to pursue golf after winning the second tournament she entered, in 1935. Three years later she married professional wrestler George Zaharias and ten years later she won her first professional golf title.

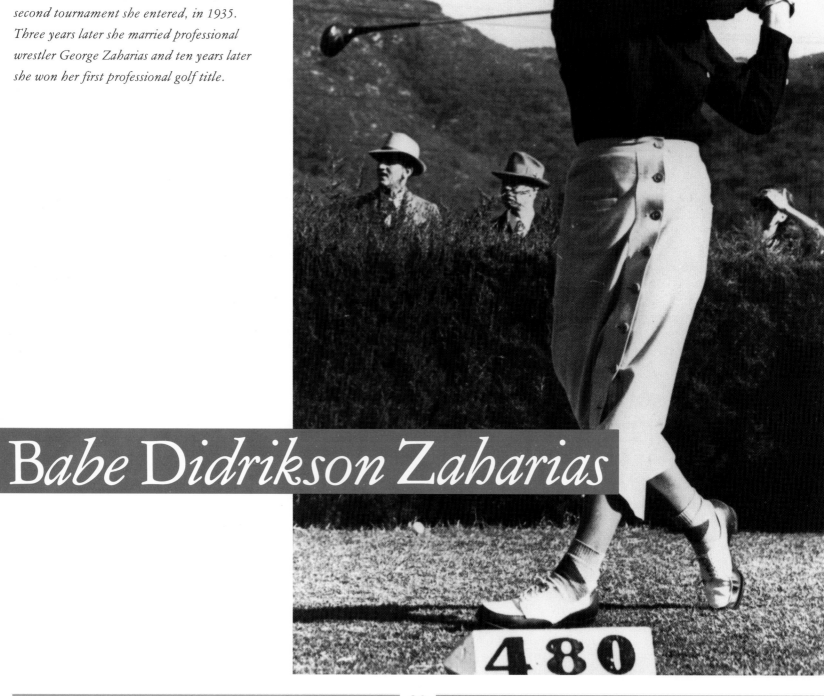

Babe Didrikson Zaharias

480

USGA Golf House

SHE WAS BORN ON JUNE 26, 1914, IN PORT ARTHUR, Texas, and became one of the world's greatest woman athletes. Mildred Didrikson could hold her own with the boys back in Texas — name the sport and she could master it.

At the age of seventeen, she participated in the American Track and Field Championships, which served as the trials for the 1932 Olympics in Los Angeles. Didrikson won six of the seven events she entered and set world records in three of them. In the Olympics, Didrikson won three events — javelin, hurdles, and high jump (although the latter title was later taken away because the headfirst leap was then considered illegal).

She was a natural. Didrikson was an All-America basketball player, a baseball and softball athlete who earned the name Babe for her epic blasts. On one occasion, she hit five home runs in one game. Swimming, diving, tennis, roller skating, and bowling came just as easily. Yet Didrikson made her greatest mark as a golfer.

It was a suggestion by sportswriter Grantland Rice that turned the twenty-one-year-old's attention to the dignified sport of golf. Didrikson won the second tournament she appeared in, the 1935 Texas Women's Invitational. But the United States Golf Association ruled her a professional after two weeks had passed, citing money she earned playing basketball and baseball. She regained her amateur standing in 1943.

She was not a textbook player by any means, but Zaharias' (she had married and taken that name) pure athletic talent was enough to overpower the opposition. She could drive the ball 250 yards off the tee. She refined the other areas of her game; Walter Hagen polished her short game; Gene Sarazen imparted his formidable knowledge of bunker play.

In 1946 and 1947, Zaharias won seventeen consecutive amateur tournaments, including the 1946 U.S. Amateur and the 1947 British Amateur. In 1948, she turned professional, and promptly won the first of three U.S. Open titles, three Women's Titleholder victories, and four Western Open championships.

Zaharias was never shy about her ability. In fact, her greatest contribution to golf was doing it her way. After her success, women stopped merely swinging gracefully at the ball, opting for distance over aesthetics. Zaharias was a pioneer, a founder of the LPGA and a leading money-winner for four consecutive years. All told, Zaharias won 31 LPGA events in the 128 events scheduled during her eight-year professional career.

In 1953, Zaharias underwent the first of two delicate operations for cancer. A year later, she won the U.S. Open at Salem Country Club in Peabody, Massachusetts. Her total of 291 was twelve strokes better than second-place finisher Betty Hicks. She died two years later.

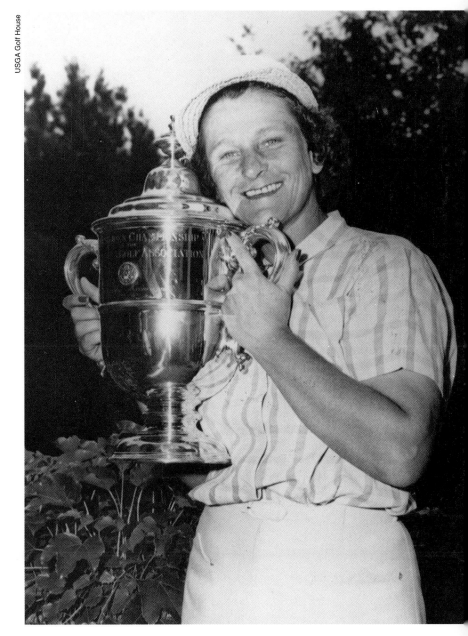

USGA Golf House

Babe was a money golfer, collecting trophies at a regular pace. She led all woman golfers in earnings her first four years as a professional.

(left) *Note the eloquent carriage, the graceful follow-through. Walter Hagen killed them softly with his fluid technique—and he didn't just look good. Hagen could play, as evidenced by his four consecutive PGA Tour championships. It was Hagen who moved the game out of Norfolk jackets and breeches and into the realm of brightly colored cardigans and those nifty two-tone shoes.*

USGA Golf House

Walter Hagen

USGA Golf House

Hagen's specialty was the recovery; this was due to his tendency to be a little wild off the tee. Nevertheless, his irons, especially the seven, eight, and nine, were the stuff of legends. Hagen would try any shot, which made him a match-play phenomenon: He won nine of ten matches in Ryder Cup play.

HE WAS FLAMBOYANT — PERHAPS THE MOST RIVETING golfer ever to grace the greens — and he could play a little golf, too. That is Walter Hagen's legacy: Spectacular style coupled with substance. Though his polka-dot bow ties, two-tone shoes, and dashing plus fours were the stuff of fashion in the vibrant 1920s, don't forget about Hagen's five PGA championships — four of them in a row, which is still a record.

More than any golfer, Hagen tore down the social barriers that had been established between amateurs and professionals, for he was the consummate pro. Born in Rochester, New York, on December 21, 1892, Hagen was not a sterling shotmaker on the order of Bobby Jones or Sam Snead. Rather, he was a master of the recovery. "The Haig's" short irons to the green — the mashie (seven iron), the mashie niblick (eight iron), and the niblick (nine iron) — usually rescued Hagen from errant drives. His putter often turned potential pars into birdies.

He learned his craft, at least initially, by watching others. Hagen left school at the age of twelve to become a full-time caddie at his local club in Rochester. Seven years later, he would turn professional. At the age of twenty, Hagen played in his first U.S. Open, which afforded him his first view of British legend Harry Vardon. Boston amateur Francis Ouimet eventually beat Vardon in a three-way playoff with Ted Ray, but Hagen came away impressed with Vardon's overwhelming presence and technique, which was a sort of studied casualness. Hagen

adopted the approach and almost seemed to walk into his shots. His wide stance caused what can only be described as an off-balance follow-through, but Hagen learned how to compensate.

He was one of the first great players to understand the value of good bunker play — perhaps because his hooks and slices left him so often in the sand. Hagen didn't have the benefit of the soon-to-be-designed sand wedge, so he finessed his recovery shots with a thin niblick. Over the years, Hagen raised the concept of getting down in two strokes to an art form.

A year after his first encounter with Vardon, Hagen won the U.S. Open (in 1914) and repeated the feat five years later. In 1921 came the first of those five PGA titles, and in 1922 Hagen won his first of four British Open championships. Though he had placed 53rd in his first Open two years earlier, Hagen would win four times, place second once, and place third once in the next seven tries. Hagen played in the first five Ryder Cup matches between the United States and Great Britain and lost only one of nine games.

It was his match play that best underlined Hagen's uncommon talent. He was a ruthless opponent, a garrulous spirit who would distract playing partners with an endless dialogue with spectators. His four consecutive victories in the PGA tournament consisted of victories in twenty-two straight games — all played over a grueling thirty-six holes.

Years of hard work on the practice tee gave birth to the swing that was considered golf's finest. Thus, Ben Hogan's success began at the relatively late age of twenty-five, when he finally won his first professional golf tournament. Eight years later, Hogan collected the first of his eight major titles. At the age of thirty-six, Hogan made one of the greatest comebacks in sports history. He survived a brutal auto accident and came back to dominate golf as never before, winning tournaments and collecting trophies (far right).

THE CAR WAS MOVING ALONG HIGHWAY 80 IN THE THICK morning fog between Fort Worth and Van Horn, Texas, when it suddenly slammed into a bus. Driver Ben Hogan threw himself toward the passenger seat, occupied by his wife, Valerie, there by saving her life. Yet Hogan's future — not to mention his formidable golfing career — was left very much in doubt. A full 90 minutes passed before Hogan was pulled from the wreckage, his legs badly mutilated, and driven 150 miles to an El Paso

Ben Hogan

hospital. The damage: A fractured pelvis, shoulder, rib, and ankle, and a life-threatening blood clot.

Eleven months later, in January, 1950, after missing most of the 1949 season, Hogan was an experimental entry at the Los Angeles Open, where he tied Sam Snead by shooting three consecutive 69s, and eventually lost in a playoff. Hogan went on to win the U.S. Open in 1950, though, an event he had captured in 1948. He repeated the feat in 1951 and 1953 also. Could he have won the title four years in a row or five times in six years if it had not been for his debilitating accident? That was the provocative golfing question of the day. Yet another "what if" question began then and still stimulates golfing conversations today.

Hogan had already won the 1953 U.S. Open and Masters, the first two legs of golfing's Grand Slam, when he made his first journey to the British Open. It was played at Carnoustie,

© Fred Roe

USGA Golf House

Scotland, and Hogan arrived two weeks early to dissect the 7,200-yard layout he had never seen before. Hogan took a lead to the final day and fired a 68 to win by four strokes, thus becoming the first, and to this day still, the only man to win the first three jewels of the Grand Slam. Travel plans home were not successful, however, and Hogan did not return from Great Britain in time to play in the PGA championship. What if? Hogan had won that tournament in 1946 and 1948, and his searing game in 1953 certainly suggested another win was possible. We will never know what might have been — Walter Burkemo beat Felice Torza two and one at Birmingham Country Club, in Michigan — save only to say that Ben Hogan was perhaps the best golfer that ever lived.

He had it all. The picture-perfect swing, the confident putting stroke, the mind that always played a stroke ahead. Hogan, born in Dublin, Texas, in 1912, was not physically gifted, but through

hours of practice he made himself a great golfer. He didn't win his first tournament until the age of twenty-five, and won his first major, the 1946 PGA, at thirty-three. Before the accident, Hogan had a low, crouching stance that produced an aggressive, sometimes slashing stroke. That approach worked for thirteen tournament victories in 1946 (second only to Byron Nelson's eighteen titles the years before) and another eleven wins in 1948. One of the fallouts of Hogan's mishap was a shortened backswing. Distance gave way to greater accuracy and his unprecedented successes of the early 1950s. He won sixty-two tournaments in all, behind only Sam Snead and Jack Nicklaus, and one ahead of Arnold Palmer.

Hogan's consistency was at times frightening. In a string of fourteen consecutive U.S. Opens and Masters, he never failed to place in the top ten. On eight of those occasions, Hogan finished in the top four.

Bobby Jones

USGA Golf House

A single accomplishment sets Bobby Jones apart from the rest of the great golfers: In 1930, he achieved the Grand Slam by winning the British and United States Amateur championships, and the British and U.S. Opens. No man, before or since, could manage that. That done, Jones retired at the age of twenty-eight. His golfing legacy survives today in the form of the Master's tournament at Augusta National, which he helped launch in 1934, playing with Paul Runyan on the first day, (right). Jones fired a four-over-par 76; Horton Smith was eventually the inaugural winner.

THOUGH HE BLAZED ACROSS THE GOLFING LANDSCAPE for a relatively brief 14-year period, Robert Tyre Jones remains golf's greatest legend.

He had a perfect swing that never seemed to come untracked, an unmatched resolve, and an ability to strike well-placed shots under pressure. He won thirteen major tournaments and was beloved on both shores of the Atlantic. What he did in 1930 probably will never be equaled.

He had already won the British Open twice, in 1926 and 1927, when he made the long journey to Hoylake, England, and beat Macdonald Smith and Leo Diegel for his third title. Jones' only British Amateur championship quickly followed on the Old Course at St. Andrews, and he was greeted as a conquering hero with a ticker-tape parade in New York City. He fired a 287 to win his fourth U.S. Open title at Interlachen Country Club in Minnesota, again edging the determined Smith. And then in the fall of 1930, Jones defeated Eugene Homans in the U.S. Amateur, marking his fifth triumph in the event. It was immediately dubbed the "Impregnable Quadrilateral" and it was every bit as amazing as its name. Jones had won golf's four major championships in a single year. (Today, the Masters tournament he developed and the PGA are considered the third and fourth legs of the Grand Slam, along with the U.S. and British Opens.)

Jones was born in Atlanta, Georgia, on March 17, 1902, and played in his first U.S. Amateur championship at the age of fourteen. He won the Georgia State Amateur that year and, one year later, the Southern Amateur championship. In 1921, Jones made the first of many trips to Great Britain. He recorded a forty-six over the first nine holes at St. Andrews, drove his tee shot at the No. 11 hole into the Eden River, and promptly tore up his scorecard.

Jones had a unique understanding of the physics involved in an effective golf swing. It was hard to determine where his power came from — he stroked the ball with an economical, well-timed swing that was built around the thrust of his hips. His swing was so rhythmic, so lyrical, that many thought it was a lazy approach to the ball. Not so. Jones' follow-through was perfect, too: Hands held low and torso turned toward the intended target.

Like other great golfers, Jones was surrounded by his share of legend and lore. His trusty putter, Calamity Jane, had an uncertain origin. It was named for the boisterous character from the old Wild West, and the hickory-shafted club with a slightly lofted blade rarely failed Jones. One story has the club coming from Long Island professional Jimmy Maiden in 1921 after Jones took a beating from Francis Ouimet in the U.S. Amateur. Another suggests Jones received the club in 1923 from one of Maiden's

young assistants, Joe Merkel, just before the U.S. Open. In any case, the shaft was broken in two places and bound with twine. It served him well over the years.

After winning the Grand Slam in 1930, Jones retired from competition at the age of twenty-eight, when he seemed to be in his prime. But Jones was already feeling the strain of winning at golf's highest levels. In 1934, he helped engineer the first Augusta National Invitation, the tournament that became the Masters.

USGA Golf House

Though he was best known for his meticulous putting style, Bobby Locke was a strong player off the tee (left). His specialty was "the draw," a method of playing the ball from right to left that is today standard procedure. His overall game was consistently superb; in head-to-head competition with Sam Snead, he won twelve of sixteen matches. Locke's victory in the 1950 British Open at Troon (right) was memorable for several reasons: He broke the tournament record by an incredible four strokes, and became only the fourth player to win successive British Open Titles. The others are Walter Hagen, James Braid, and Bobby Jones.

Bobby Locke

DRIVE FOR SHOW, BOBBY LOCKE ONCE SAID, BUT PUTT for dough. And he practiced what he preached: Bobby Locke quite possibly may have been the leading practitioner of the gentle, cerebral art of putting.

Born Arthur d'Arcy, Locke was not a particularly strong man, but he was one of the first players to consistently draw the ball, or play it from right to left. This was a characteristic even of his skilled putting stroke. When Locke was at the height of his game, in the 1940s and 1950s, putting had become a more important facet of the game. Greens became larger and smoother and players generally had grown more adept at reaching them. Putting had become the skill that separated the men from the boys.

Locke's routine was always the same. He would walk along the line of the putt, picking away any foreign material that might be in the way. He would bend over the hole, left hand holding the putter, right hand on his knee, and study the last several feet of the potential path of the ball. That done, Locke would stride back to the ball, squat behind it, putter stretched out toward the hole. Two practice swings later, Locke was ready to have a go at it. His overlapping grip had a unique twist: Both thumbs ran down the top of the shaft instead of being placed on either side, as was the convention of the time. Locke would swing through the ball, placing topspin on it by keeping his hands moving through the same plane. This strict form was always maintained and would influence several generations, for Locke's concentration was impenetrable. Even a six-inch putt merited this involved procedure.

Born in Germiston, Transvaal, to parents who had just emigrated to South Africa from Ireland, Locke won his first South African Open title at the age of eighteen. He would win eight more championships and enjoy a twenty-year stretch when he was unbeaten over seventy-two holes in his native country. During World War II, Locke served as a bomber pilot in the South African Air Force. Later, in a series of sixteen challenge matches in South Africa, Locke managed to beat the great Sam Snead twelve times. The American champion urged Locke to visit America and play the tour there.

In 1947, the first of Locke's two years in the United States, he won six of the thirteen tournaments he played in, placed second twice, and never finished lower than seventh. For a three-tournament period, Locke was unbeatable. Today, he is one of only eleven players to win three straight. In 1948, Locke played in twenty-five tournaments, in which he won twice, finished second twice, and missed the top ten only three times. But golf in America wasn't for him.

Locke won his first British Open at Royal St. George's in 1949 with a playoff triumph over Harry Bradshaw and repeated the following year at Troon in Scotland with an easier victory over Roberto DeVicenzo. In 1952, Locke won his third Open title in four years at Royal Lytham. In 1957, at the age of thirty-nine, Locke ended a three-year run by Peter Thomson for his fourth British Open title. Nine years, four championships. During that incredible span, Locke won the Egyptian Open, the French Open, the German Open, the Irish Open, the Mexican Open, and the Swiss Open, among others.

Nancy Lopez

She arrived at a time (1977) when ladies' golf was just beginning to blaze across the consciousness of the American sporting public. After placing second in one of six tournaments that initial year, Lopez won nine tournaments in 1978, including a record five in a row. Not only was she Rookie of the Year, Lopez was Player of the Year. She continued her golfing dominance (winning, among other tournaments, the 1980 Kemper Open, left) and remains a star today.

PRECOCIOUS WASN'T THE WORD FOR NANCY LOPEZ: IT was more like ferocious. She was the New Mexico Women's Amateur champion at the age of twelve. When she turned fifteen, Nancy Lopez won the U.S.G.A. Junior Girls title for the first time, then repeated again in 1973 and 1974. She won her first LPGA tournament at the age of twenty-one. Nine years later, Lopez was inducted into the LPGA Hall of Fame.

Lopez is the modern phenomenon who helped make women's golf a viable sporting enterprise. Since she began playing, in 1977, LPGA purses have nearly quadrupled, to an astounding $11 million for the year of 1987, and Nancy Lopez, whose sparkling personality is matched only by her competitive nature, is the most obvious reason the sport has grown so popular.

Born January 6, 1957, in Torrance, California, Lopez learned golf at the age of eight from her father, Domingo, and immediately started winning every amateur tournament in sight.

The great strength of Lopez' game is its well-rounded nature. Equally adept at making the pressure putts (right) as well as the long drives off the tee (left), Lopez seems destined for even more success. Through it all, she has maintained that her full-time job as mother of two and husband to baseball's Ray Knight is just as important as her career in golf.

© Bill Knight/Pro Photo Inc.

As an All-America golfer at Tulsa University in 1976, her sophomore year, Lopez decided to turn professional.

She played in only six tournaments in 1977, winning a total of $23,138 and finishing as high as second place (for her first money, in the Colgate European Open). Technically, Lopez was still a rookie during the 1978 season. It's just that she played like a steely veteran. There has never been another year like it in the annals of golf. Lopez played in twenty-five tournaments and won nine of them, including the LPGA Championship at Jack Nicklaus Golf Club in King's Island, Ohio. Lopez shot a thirteen-under-par 275 to beat Amy Alcott by six strokes. From May 12th to June 18th, Lopez won five straight tournaments she appeared in. Lopez won a total of $189,813, a new standard for rookies. Her stroke average of 71.76 was another record, and left her as the uncontested LPGA Player of the Year. She was, of course, the Rookie of the Year as well.

And then she did it all over again. In 1979, Lopez won $197,488 to lead all LPGA golfers and took home eight tournament titles. Her stroke average of 71.20 was a new LPGA record until she herself broke it in 1985.

Lopez was married in 1982 to baseball player Ray Knight, the Mets' third baseman who would become the Most Valuable Player in the World Series in 1986. In 1983 (despite an interruption due to pregnancy) Lopez became the fifth LPGA player to earn $1 million when she tied for sixth in the Nabisco Dinah Shore. Playing part-time while bringing up daughter Ashley Marie, Lopez played in 16 tournaments in 1984 before having the year of her career in 1985.

Her consistency was amazing. Lopez played in twenty-five tournaments and placed in the top ten twenty-one times. She recorded five victories, including another LPGA Championship title. There was a string of twelve consecutive top-five finishes. Lopez finished the season with $416,472 in winnings, becoming the first LPGA golfer to surpass $400,000. She also added another $125,000, plus two automobiles for capturing the spring and summer segments of the Mazda-LPGA Series. Not surprisingly, Lopez' scoring average of 70.73 was another record. Her play in the Henredon Classic was unearthly. At the Willow Creek Golf Club in High Point, North Carolina, Lopez shot 66—67—69—66 for a record twenty-under-par 268. The twenty-five birdies Lopez recorded were also a new LPGA mark. Lopez won the Vare Trophy and Play of the Year honors, each for the third time, then took off most of 1986 to devote time to having her second child, Erinn Shea.

As a golfer and as a mother, Nancy Lopez always did things on her own terms. Considering that she started her career so early, there is no telling what Lopez may yet accomplish.

USGA Golf House

FORGET FOR A MOMENT (IF YOU CAN) THE ELEVEN straight tournaments that Byron Nelson won in 1945, because he achieved an even more remarkable feat: During his career Nelson never, ever, finished over par in a four-round tournament. That makes him the most consistent golfer in history.

Nelson was born on February 4, 1912, in Fort Worth, Texas, and was brought up there on the edge of the Glen Country Club. By the age of ten, Nelson was caddying for members. He won his

Byron Nelson

first amateur tournament in 1930 at the age of eighteen. In 1935, while an assistant golf professional, Nelson won the New Jersey State Open. Two years later, while still an unknown talent, Nelson won the 1937 Masters. That same year he was fifth in the British Open to Henry Cotton at Muirfield, having arrived earlier as a member of the American Ryder Cup team. In 1939, Nelson won his first and only U.S. Open championship in a double playoff. He and Craig Wood fired 68s to eliminate Denny Shute after eighteen extra holes. Then Nelson put Wood away on the No. 4 hole at Philadelphia Country Club with an eagle two and went on to win by three strokes. It was, Nelson maintains, the best shot of his career.

Nelson was not exactly a stylist, but he got the job done. His putting tended to be erratic, but his irons were the best part of his game. He was accurate to the green with all of them and that served to reinforce his bold nature. Nelson was always swinging at the flag.

If there is a criticism of Nelson, it is that his greatest glories came during the war years, when the field were not as strong as they could have been. On the other hand, if the U.S. Open hadn't been suspended between 1942 and 1945, or if the Masters had been played from 1943 to 1945, or the British Open had been contested during its five-year sabbatical, surely Nelson would have won far more than his five major tournaments. As it was, Nelson had to be content with dominating the regular tour.

In 1944, Nelson entered twenty-three tournaments and won eight of them. And then, in 1945, Nelson dominated golf in a way no player ever matched, before or since. He entered thirty-one tournaments and won eighteen — a PGA record. Eleven of those victories came consecutively, during an incredible span from March 8 at the Miami Four Ball to the Canadian Open on August 4. Included during that magnificent run was one of

Nelson's two PGA titles. There was actually a twelfth tournament victory during that time, but the Spring Lake, New Jersey, purse of $2,500 wasn't up to the PGA's standard of $3,000. Nelson's total take from the five-month period was $30,250. Today, such a tear would be worth more than a million. His scoring average, buoyed by a series of nineteen consecutive rounds under 70, was a ridiculous 68.33.

In all, Nelson won fifty-four tournaments. He retired in his prime, just after the 1945 season. He played intermittently afterward, and won the 1955 Paris Open. In 1965, he captained the U.S. Ryder Cup team at Royal Birkdale. After that, Nelson became a broadcaster, and demonstrated his thorough knowledge of golf. And long after his active playing days were over, Nelson was still a force on the PGA Tour. Tom Watson, who would win five British Open titles in a nine-year span, was Nelson's personal protégé.

It wasn't Byron Nelson's fault that he chose to dominate the sport of golf at a time when many would-be athletes were fighting overseas. If World War II had never happened, chances are Nelson would have fared quite nicely—and won his share of the twelve major tournaments that were suspended during that time. Even in his later years, (right) Nelson was something of a fixture on the golfing scene. He appeared on television and at clinics, stressing the game's fundamentals. Tom Watson, one of history's best golfers, was only one of those who took his techniques to heart. Over the years, Nelson and Watson became quite close, which made Watson's triumphs in four Byron Nelson Classics, from 1975–80, something special.

IT IS A MEASURE OF JACK NICKLAUS' TRULY GREAT determination that once he decided golf's major championships were his most important goal, he went out and won more than any golfer in history. Mere recital of these staggering accomplishments fails to convey their grandeur: Through 1986, Nicklaus had won six Masters titles, five PGA championships, four U.S. Opens, three British Opens, and two U.S. Amateurs.

Imagine that. Yet it was evident very early on that Nicklaus would become one of the most successful golfers in history. He was born on January 21, 1940, in Columbus, Ohio, and received his first lesson at age ten from a professional named Jack Grout. Within five years, Nicklaus had qualified for the U.S. Amateur championship. At the age of nineteen, Nicklaus became the second-youngest winner of that celebrated tournament, taking it in 1959 and then again in 1961. That was his last year as an amateur and he went out in style, winning the 1961 N.C.A.A. championship while a student at Ohio State.

Nicklaus, who had placed second to Arnold Palmer in the 1960 U.S. Open at Cherry Hills Country Club in Denver, locked up with Palmer in 1962 at Oakmont Country Club in

Jack Nicklaus

It took Nicklaus some time to endear himself to golfing audiences. But by the time Arnold Palmer had begun to slow down, Nicklaus became the sport's leading figure. From 1962, when he turned professional, through 1978, he never finished lower than fourth on the PGA Tour's money list. When he first arrived on the golf scene in 1959, Nicklaus was an overweight athlete with a blond crewcut who could hit the ball out of sight. He won the U.S. Amateur championship in 1959, then won the NCAA and U.S. Amateur titles in 1961 before turning professional.

© Fred Roe

Pennsylvania. They both shot 283 over the first four rounds to force a playoff. In one corner was Palmer, at the height of his game and popularity. In the other corner stood Nicklaus, he of the blond crewcut, overweight physique, and relentless approach. Most of America was hoping Palmer would teach the "Golden Bear" a lesson, but it happened the other way around. Nicklaus fired a 71, compared to Palmer's 74, and won his first major at the age of twenty-two.

Nicklaus's game never relied heavily on subtlety — he was one of the game's first power brokers — but over the years his short game became more and more polished. And as he grew his hair and trimmed a few extra pounds, he became as beloved

as Palmer had been. The world loves a winner and Nicklaus delivered again and again.

Consider Nicklaus's major championship record: He won eighteen titles and placed second another eighteen times, with nine third-place finishes. Over a span of twenty-three years, from 1962 to 1984, there were only two years when Nicklaus didn't win or place second in a major tournament. In ninety-two consecutive appearances over that time, Nicklaus placed in the top ten sixty-seven times.

Through 1986, Nicklaus had won seventy-one tournaments and placed second fifty-eight times. Only Sam Snead (eighty-four victories) won more. Nicklaus, however, was fortunate to

As the years passed, Nicklaus (below, *flanked by rival Tom Watson and President Gerald Ford*) grew into his role as golf's leading ambassador. He was greatly responsible for golf's flowering in the 1970s and later developed a talent for designing golf courses. Accompanied by his ever-present caddie, Angelo (right), Nicklaus lines up one of his many critical career putts. He never seemed to lose his touch, either. After winning the Colonial National Invitation in 1982, many critics thought his competitive career was over. Not so. He won the Memorial in 1984; then, at age forty-six, Nicklaus won the 1986 Masters.

© R. Mackson/FPG Intl.

play in an age when golfers were compensated better for their talents. From the time he joined the PGA Tour, in 1962, through 1978, Nicklaus placed among the top four money-winners every year. He led all players eight different times and was the second golfer to pass the $1-million mark (1970), the first to reach the $2-million mark (1973), the $3-million mark (1977), the $4-million mark (1983), and the $5-million mark (1987).

Only three other golfers in history have managed to win each of the major championships at least once — Gene Sarazen, Ben Hogan, and Gary Player. They all completed the set once each. Nicklaus has done it three times over. In 1972, he fell two shots short of holding all four titles during the same year.

In 1986, at the age of forty-six, Nicklaus won his most popular victory. He hadn't won a tournament in two years, but on the back nine at Augusta National, Nicklaus summoned strength from somewhere deep in his past. He played the last ten holes in seven under par to shoot a 65 on the fourth day for a one-stroke victory over Greg Norman and Tom Kite.

WITH GOLF CAUGHT IN AN IDENTITY CRISIS IN THE MIDDLE 1980s (those mechanical, long-hitting blonds all looked alike, some said) Greg Norman was considered the next Great Thing, the possible bear apparent to Jack Nicklaus's throne.

As Nicklaus himself says, "Greg Norman has all the tools to be the greatest player in the game. He can adjust to any course."

The main tool is Norman's 6-foot-1, 185-pound frame, which seems sculpted for the peculiar purpose of striking golf balls. Although didn't pick up a club until the age of sixteen, when he first caddied for his mother, in two years, Norman went from a twenty-seven-handicapper to scratch. It was Nicklaus,

© Bruce Mathews/Mathews Communications

indirectly, who gave Norman the knowledge to succeed. Two of Nicklaus's books, *55 Ways to Play Golf* and *Golf My Way*, provided Norman with the basics. He took it from there.

Now, the man they call the Great White Shark strides over the global golfing terrain like Crocodile Dundee, a fellow Australian. Norman is truly an international hero: In 1980 he won the French Open, the Australian Open, the Scandinavian Open, and the Suntory World Match Play. Norman finished fourth in the 1981 Masters, and his fishing tales describing shark hunts drew national attention. He officially joined the PGA Tour in 1983 and in 1986 fulfilled his great promise.

He won the British Open at Turnberry, Scotland, and in nineteen tournaments placed in the top ten on ten different occasions. Norman won the Panasonic–Las Vegas Invitational and the Kemper Open to finish as the Tour's leading money-winner, but it was his second-place finishes that had people comparing him to the legendary Bobby Jones. It was in 1930 that Jones won the big four: The British Open and Amateur championships, and the U.S. Open and Amateur championships. (Today, the Masters and the PGA tournament have replaced the two amateur championships on the Grand Slam agenda.)

In 1986, incredibly, Norman led all four tournaments heading into the final round. Nicklaus won the Masters by playing the last ten holes in seven under par. Norman faltered in the U.S. Open at Shinnecock Hills Golf Club in New York, placing twelfth behind winner Ray Floyd. The PGA appeared to be Norman's up to the last hole. That was when mild-mannered Bob Tway holed an impossible thirty-foot bunker shot to beat Norman by a stroke.

His historically unprecedented luck continued the following year at the Masters. Before Tway's blast, no one had ever won one of golf's major championships, in 127 years of play, by sinking a shot from off the last green. And then it happened again. At Augusta Country Club, Norman found himself tied in a playoff with local boy Larry Mize. From a difficult position to the right of the eleventh green, Mize hit a sand wedge about ninety feet that bounced twice in the fringe and rolled fifty feet, curling left, and into the hole. No one, including Mize, could believe it.

"Two incredible shots," Norman says. "And two second-place finishes. I've got to find strength from that. When you're in the hunt like that, you know you're going to win eventually."

Greg Norman

Sadly, history's lingering memory of Greg Norman may be one of frustration. In 1986, he was a round away from winning all four Grand Slam titles. Although he went on to win the British Open, he faded in the U.S. Open, lost the Masters to Jack Nicklaus, and lost the PGA to Bob Tway.

© Jim Moriarty

HIS WAS NOT A CAREER BASED ON CONSISTENT brilliance or longevity, yet Francis Ouimet made a lasting impression. It was Ouimet, as a twenty-year-old amateur, who, oddly enough, put professional golfing on the map in America in the 1920s.

Around the turn of the century, the U.S. Open was considered a poor man's version of the U.S. Amateur. It had been inaugurated in 1895 and won that year by Horace Rawlins, the

Francis Ouimet

home professional at Newport Golf Club in Rhode Island. In truth, Rawlins was a British import who early on grasped the potential hold golfing might have over America. His rounds of 45, 46, 41, and 41 bested Willie Dunn over the nine-hole layout.

In 1900, Harry Vardon gave the U.S. Open a new credibility. The British star had already won three Opens in his own country, and now he showed another continent how it was done. The famous overlapping Vardon grip helped propel him to a winning total of 313 at the Chicago Golf Club, two better than J.H. Taylor. It was thirteen years before Vardon would make the long ocean journey again. In the meantime, Scotsman Willie Anderson won four titles in five years, while Alex Smith and John McDermott, the first American-born champion, won two each.

In 1913, Vardon entered the U.S. Open field at The Country Club in Brookline, Massachusetts. With him came reigning British Open champion Ted Ray; the two were made co-favorites. The pre-tournament predictions came to pass when Vardon and Ray shot 304 to finish tied at the end of seventy-two regulation holes. With them, however, was Francis Ouimet.

Years earlier, Ouimet had been a caddy at Brookline, but had since moved on to become a member of the nearby Woodland club. That he reached a three-way playoff with Vardon (ultimately a six-time winner in the British Open) and Ray was incredible enough. That he had a chance to win was out of the realm of possibility. Vardon wrote in his later days that he and Ray were concerned only with each other. Ouimet, of course, was thinking only of himself.

Vardon bested Ray by a single shot, 77 to 78, but Ouimet fired a 72 for the title and one of sport's greatest upsets. Many experts consider that moment critical for golf in the United States. The world loves an underdog and here was one of David-and-Goliath proportions. If Ouimet could do it, who couldn't?

Although Walter Hagen won at Midlothian Country Club in

Illinois a year later, and was followed by people like Gene Sarazan, Bobby Jones, and Jack Nicklaus, it was Ouimet who helped make the game popular and gave it a new respect. Ray would win the U.S. Open title in 1920 at Inverness Country Club in Toledo, Ohio. Vardon was right behind him, tied for second. Ouimet never came close to his national championship again, though he became the U.S. Amateur champion a year later and then again in 1931. Ouimet also played in every Walker Cup match from 1922 to 1949, either as a player or a captain. Still, his influence on the professional game had been felt.

Since Ray's victory, only one English player — Tony Jacklin in 1970 — has managed to win the trophy that had once seemed to belong to the British empire. The people across the water understood Ouimet's contribution. In 1951, he became the first non-British golfer to be honored as captain of the Royal and Ancient at St. Andrews.

Many people, including Willie Anderson, Alex Smith, and Ralph Guldahl, won more United States Opens than Francis Ouimet, but his place in golf history is probably more secure. As a twenty-year-old amateur in 1913, Ouimet beat heavily favored British professionals Harry Vardon and Ted Ray to win the U.S. Open at The Country Club in Brookline, Massachusetts. The game was never quite the same in the U.S. after that.

USGA Golf House

USGA Golf House

NEVER ON A GOLF COURSE HAS THERE WALKED A MORE blatantly aggressive man than Arnold Daniel Palmer. He was pretty aggressive off the course, too.

Palmer introduced the word "charge" to golf, a sport that had previously prided itself on a sort of muscular grace. He was not a graceful golfer, which might be why thousands of spectators considered themselves part of Arnie's Army, that vast crowd that followed Palmer's progress through golf's most important era. It was Palmer's reckless abandon that attracted the casual sporting fan who might not otherwise have embraced such a

genteel pastime. He tugged at the glove on his left hand, hitched his trousers, steeled himself, and went to work, while the television cameras were watching.

Palmer was born in Latrobe, Pennsylvania, on September 10, 1929, the son of a professional golfer. Over the years, he developed a certain skill around the golf course, attending Wake Forest University and eventually joining the U.S. Coast Guard. He remained in the service until he was twenty-four. A year later, while he was working as a manufacturer's agent in Cleveland, Palmer managed to find time to win the 1954 U.S. Amateur

Charge! *Under that heading in the dictionary is a small picture of Arnold Palmer hitching up his trousers—or at least there should be. Time was when golf was a gentle, sleepy sport, and interest in the game was confined mostly to private clubs and the few knowledgeable fans. That changed when Palmer joined the PGA Tour in 1955. By coincidence, television was just beginning to focus its long lens on the splendor in the grass. Arnie was simply a made-for-television extravaganza just waiting to be discovered. Palmer learned the game from his father in Latrobe, Pennsylvania, but no one is quite sure where all that determination came from. Note the aggressive follow-through (right). It wasn't pretty, but something in that slashing stroke stirred the imagination of golf fans everywhere.*

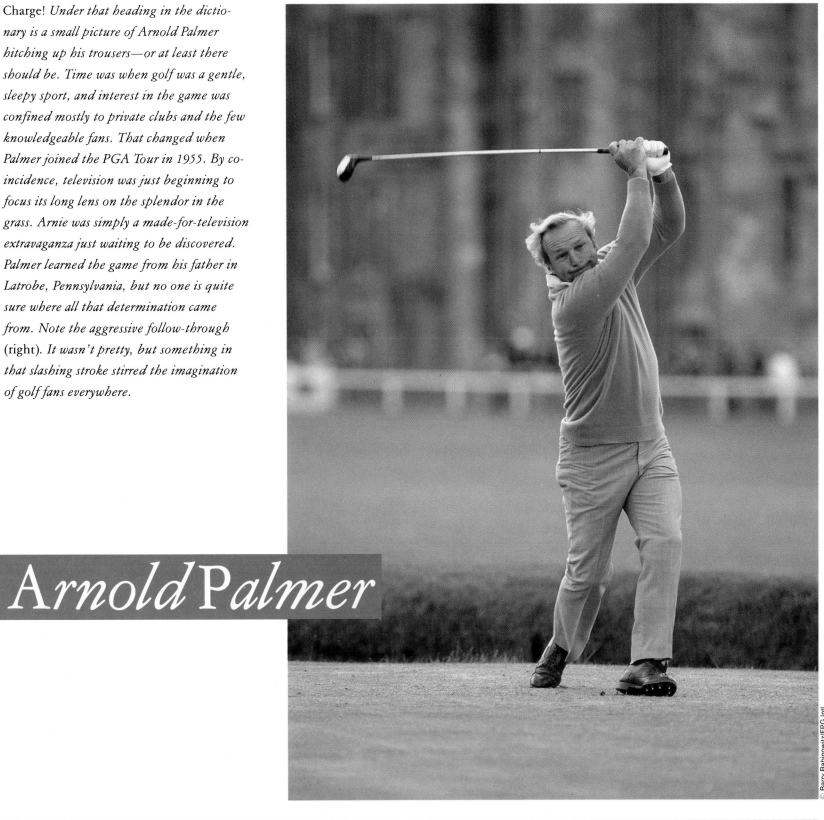

Arnold Palmer

Palmer was golf's first jet-setter. He flew his own plane, then stepped off and stepped off and beat everyone in sight. Here, he arrives in London (below) with his wife, Winifred, in 1961 for a 10,000-pound, winner-take-all match with Gary Player on the famed St. Andrews Golf Course.

© PHOTOWORLD/FPG Intl.

championship. That was enough to convince him that a professional career might be worth attempting.

In 1958, Palmer won the first of his four Masters tournaments in consecutive even-numbered years. At Augusta, Palmer threw together his first notable charge; he birdied each of the last three holes to beat Ken Venturi by a single stroke. Later that year, at the Cherry Hills Country Club in Denver, Palmer won his first and only U.S. Open championship. He trailed leader Mike Souchack by seven strokes at the beginning of the final round, but played the first nine holes in thirty strokes — by making birdies on six of the first seven holes. Palmer won, going away with a 65 and a two-stroke victory.

It was Palmer who brought new American interest to the British Open. He played first in the 100th British Open at St. Andrews, Scotland, and lost to Australia's Ken Nagle by a stroke. Palmer returned to Royal Birkdale in 1961 and won the tournament. He repeated a year later at Troon in Scotland. Palmer's career in the British Open — two firsts and a second in three times — is unmatched for its brilliance.

Palmer won sixty-one tournaments and earned a total of $1,891,020 in his twenty-six years on the PGA Tour. More importantly, he gave golf a new image, bringing it into a new and exciting age. He traveled from tournament to tournament in his private jet, signed with agent Mark McCormack, and became golf's first millionaire. Palmer, then, was the role model for golf's élite. Jack Nicklaus was only one of many golfers who owed some of their success to Palmer's trailblazing. When a player wins the money title on the PGA Tour, he is, fittingly, honored with the Palmer Award.

Palmer's game had technical shortcomings. He rounded his shoulders and crouched too severely over the ball, with his knees bent in at an alarming angle. His tremendous wrists permitted him these minor deviations from the norm. His heart, however, had the stuff of champions.

DETERMINATION, THY NAME IS GARY PLAYER.

He won his first British Open in 1959, collected another in 1968, and added a third title in 1974. That span of fifteen years between British Open victories was the longest since J.H. Taylor's nineteen-year run and the eighteen years that encompassed Harry Vardon's first and last championships. Player to this day is the only non-American golfer to win the British Open, the U.S. Open, the Masters, and the PGA Championship. (Gene Sarazen, Ben Hogan, and Jack Nicklaus are the others.) His Masters titles were similarly spread out, coming in 1961, 1974, and 1978. Player's PGA victories came in 1962 and 1972 and his lone U.S. Open triumph was in 1965. Incredibly, Player just missed a third PGA title in 1984, when he finished second to Lee Trevino.

Player's remarkable grit and longevity carried him to a second U.S. Open title in 1987, at the Brooklawn Country Club in Fairfield, Connecticut. This time, however, it was a senior tour victory. Player, a 5-foot-7, 152-pound physical fitness fanatic of fifty-one years, shot a seventy-two-hole seniors record of 270 (14-under-par) to beat second-place finisher Doug Sanders by six strokes.

"I feel like a guy of twenty-five," said Player, who looked the part. "When you've worked as hard and been as dedicated to something as I have, that's when you appreciate something like this so much. I'm just so very grateful, because I didn't have it easy when I was growing up. My father was a gold miner who worked twelve to fifteen thousand feet underground and never made $250 a month in his life. My mother died when I was eight, and my brother fought in World War II and Korea."

It was never easy. Player never established the consistency of Nicklaus and Palmer, who along with Player made up golfing's "Big Three" in the 1960s and 1970s. Still, his tenacity was admirable. In 1978, Player found himself down seven strokes to Hubert Green in the final round of the Masters. He had won the tournament at Augusta for the first time seventeen years previously, but he fired a torrid 64 to win the championship. The following week, at the Tournament of Champions, Player erased a seven-shot deficit to Seve Ballesteros in the last round and won by two strokes.

Through 1986, Player — a truly global presence — had won 128 tournaments around the world. He has flown more miles in pursuit of victory than any golfer in history. A native of Johannesburg, Player has won the South African Open thirteen times since 1956, the Australian Open seven times, and the Suntory World Match Play tournament five times.

It was his brother Ian who first instilled the physical fitness urge, pushing him to do pushups to the point of exhaustion at an early age. Player didn't take a golf club in hand until the relatively late age of fifteen, and turned professional two years later. He made himself a champion through hours of hard work and practice.

"You can never," Gary Player says, "work hard enough." The spectacular results back him up.

Gary Player

© Bill Knight/Pro Photo Inc.

© Fred Roe

He was not a big man, but early in life Gary Player learned how to get the most from his 5-foot-7, 152-pound frame. That fanatical devotion to fitness resulted in terrific finishes, even after the age of fifty. Through 1986, he had won 128 tournaments around the world.

EUGENE SARACENI WASN'T BUILT ALONG THE LINES OF today's lean-and-mean professional golfers. He was, truthfully, a little on the squat side. Yet what Gene Sarazen lacked in size he more than compensated for with determination and a graceful longevity that has never been equaled.

Born on February 27, 1902, in Harrison, New York, Sarazen soon changed his name from Saraceni because he didn't like the way it sounded. As fate would have it, Sarazen suffered from failing health that demanded a healthy hobby. Golf was his salvation. Sarazen took to it immediately; his strong upper body provided the power, and his resilient mind harnessed it.

In 1922, Sarazen became the second-youngest winner on the PGA Tour with a terrific victory over Bobby Jones and John Black in the U.S. Open at Skokie Country Club in Illinois. (Johnny McDermott had won the U.S. Open at the age of nineteen years, ten months.) Sarazen's victory was no fluke, because he followed that up with a win in the PGA championship. In 1923, Sarazen repeated, beating Walter Hagen and handing him his only defeat in the first of five successive match-play finals.

Later in 1923, Sarazan journeyed to Troon, Scotland, for the British Open, on the heels of his successes in America. He failed to qualify by a mere stroke. Five years later, Sarazen placed second to Hagen at Royal St. George's, then tied for third in 1931. He finally won the British Open title for the first and last

Gene Sarazen

time in 1932 when he teamed with his old caddie at Prince's. Sarazen used his intellectual command of the game — he is credited with inventing the sand wedge — to beat MacDonald Smith by a total of five strokes. After studying the long, dry links at Prince's, Sarazen eschewed his driver in favor of his more accurate irons. His record final score of 283 stood for seventeen years. Later that summer, Sarazen won the U.S. Open for the second time, playing his last twenty-eight holes at Fresh Meadow, New York, in an even 100 strokes.

In 1935, at age thirty-three, Sarazen struck one of golf's most famous blows. He was trailing Craig Wood by three strokes on the last day of the Masters when he teed off on the par-five No. 15 hole at Augusta. His drive of 260 yards left him 240 yards from the green, but Sarazen pulled out a number-four wood and stroked the ball over the lake in front of the green. It bounced twice and disappeared into the hole for a "golden eagle." Wood's lead disappeared, and Sarazen went on to win by five strokes in the two-round playoff. And so Sarazen became the first golfer to capture the Masters, the U.S. Open, the PGA, and the British Open.

Sarazen never seemed to lose his touch. At age fifty-six, Sarazen was able to navigate the British Open course at Royal Lytham with an average of four strokes per hole. Two years later, at the Old Course at St. Andrews, Sarazen fired a 69. At age seventy-one, Sarazen was one of the favored guests invited to Troon, Scotland, by the Royal and Ancient Golf Club of St. Andrews. Fifty years earlier Sarazen had made his disastrous debut on the very same course, but in 1973 he shot one-under the first day, including an eagle on the No. 8 hole.

USGA Golf House

Even fifty years later (left), people were asking Gene Sarazen about his famous golden eagle. It happened in 1935, when, trailing Craig Wood by three strokes in the second Masters tournament, Sarazen knocked a number-four wood into the fifteenth hole from 240 yards away. Sarazen would win by five strokes in a two-round playoff, but the eagle was the shot that made it all possible.

NO MAN HAS WON MORE GOLF TOURNAMENTS THAN SAM Snead. Through 1986, Snead's eighty-four official PGA Tour victories far outdistanced the seventy-one by Jack Nicklaus, sixty-two by Ben Hogan, and sixty-one by Arnold Palmer. Overall, Snead won 135 tournaments, not including thirty wins in regional events. Regardless of the precise figure, Snead's body of work represents thirty years of consistent, unparalleled excellence.

Although his background didn't suggest he would become a champion, Snead made himself a winner with two old standards: Practice and determination. Born in Hot Springs, Virginia, on May 27, 1912, Snead's start in golf was hardly auspicious — he cleaned the clubs and shoes of the members at the Cascades

Sam Snead

Inn Club, then walked (in properly heroic fashion) three miles to his home. He had seen his brother, Homer, cracking golf balls in a meadow adjacent to the Snead household and by age seven was experimenting with a piece of maple with a knot at the end.

Snead began to caddy at the Homestead Course, but he wasn't big enough to carry bags and was demoted to shopboy. Eventually, Snead returned to Cascades as an assistant professional, where he put together a varied collection of clubs. It was there that a local businessman named Fred Martin prevailed on Snead to pursue golf as a career. The hours of practice with that splinter of maple had made the mechanics of the swing seem almost second nature to Snead, and success came rapidly.

He turned professional in 1934 and began winning titles with his natural "feeling-the-club" swing. In the late 1930s, Snead began two streaks that would underline his ability to grind out victory after victory. In 1938, he won the Greater Greensboro Open for the first of eight times — a PGA Tour record for wins in a single event. He managed the feat over a twenty-seven-year period. Snead is also second in the record books, winning the Miami Open six times between 1937 and 1955.

Snead won his first major tournament, the PGA, in 1942 at Seaview Country Club in Atlantic City, New Jersey, besting Jim Turnesa 2 and 1 in the match-play final. He won the PGA title again in 1949 and 1952, the British Open at St. Andrews, Scotland in 1946, and the Masters at Augusta three different times (1949, 1952, 1954). There is a good possibility that Snead

Sam Snead started cranking out the victories in the mid-1930s, and snowballed through the 1940s and 1950s—and 1960s. Snead's swing (below) *had a balance and grace that carried it through the years.*

USGA Golf House

As the years passed, so did Snead's putting nerve. Always the innovator, Snead eventually embraced this distinctive side-saddle putting style (right) *because, he said, it made him feel more comfortable. Don't laugh—he won numerous tournaments with this unconventional stroke. Snead's ability to play well when others around him gave into old age was remarkable. In 1985, Snead shot his age or better fourteen times, including a dazzling 68 in the final round of the Syracuse Seniors. In 1986, Snead shot his age— 74—in all four rounds of the Greater Grand Rapids Seniors event.*

would have been considered the greatest golfer of all time, ahead of Jack Nicklaus, if he had been able to capture the fourth major, the U.S. Open.

Much has been made of Snead's remarkable failures in that pursuit. He was a second-place finisher four different times. In 1939, Snead needed only a five on the final hole at Philadelphia, but shot an eight. In 1947, Snead finished in a tie with Lew Worsham at St. Louis, then missed a thirty-inch playoff putt.

Still, Snead played for a remarkable length of time. He won his last tournament, his final Greensboro Open, at age fifty-two. On the 1985 Senior Tour, the seventy-three-year-old Snead shot his age or better fourteen times, including a final round of 68 in the Syracuse Seniors. His sidesaddle putting style was the only visible concession to advancing age. In 1986, at the age of seventy-four, Snead shot his age or better in every round of the Greater Grand Rapids Seniors.

HIS CLASSROOM WAS A PUBLIC COURSE IN TEXAS AND his instrument was a heavily taped Dr. Pepper bottle. Lee Trevino would bet any pigeon he could find: "I can beat you and your full bag of clubs with this 'ol bottle." He could and he did.

Thus did Trevino, the hustler, learn his art. Over the years it flourished, and by the end of 1987, Trevino had won twenty-seven titles, including six majors. Only Jack Nicklaus and Tom Watson have won more money than his $3 million career earnings. Oddly enough, it is Trevino's personality that will endure.

"I'm just a merry Mexican," Trevino would say. But he was more than that. Trevino was a refreshing breeze in a sometimes stale game that often took itself too seriously. Before the last round of a U.S. Open, paired with Nicklaus, Trevino shocked (and delighted) the Golden Bear with the old rubber-snake-in-

Lee Trevino

the-golf-bag trick. The tension was broken and both players went on to stroke some of their best shots. He was a nonstop talker, who barely paused long enough to hit the ball. Sometimes, he seemed to hit it on the run.

Trevino could play, too.

Technically, he turned pro in 1960, at age twenty-one. It wasn't until six years later, however, that Trevino made his first important impression. It was only a fifty-fourth-place finish in the U.S. Open at Olympic Country Club, but the next year at Baltusrol, in New Jersey, he was sixth. Trevino's Texas golf game depended heavily on accurate tee shots; his low drives held up best on tight, wind-whipped courses. Once on the green, Trevino would putt from the gut. In 1968, the relative unknown continued his progression in the U.S. Open at Oak Hill Country Club — he won it with a spectacular series of four consecutive rounds in the 60s, something no other man has done.

When Trevino found himself tied with Nicklaus after four rounds in the 1971 U.S. Open at Merion, everybody knew who he was. He defeated Nicklaus in the playoff and began a five-week run that may never be equaled. Trevino won the Canadian Open and then the British Open at Royal Birkdale. Only Bobby Jones, Gene Sarazen, and Ben Hogan managed to win the U.S. and British Opens back to back. It was Trevino's best year ever.

Trevino's guile under pressure was evident a year later at Muirfield, when he snatched the British Open championship

from local favorite Tony Jacklin. Incredibly, Trevino holed three delicate chips and a bunker blast to take the lead on the second-to-last hole. From 1970 to 1972, Trevino was the game's low scorer, winning the Vardon Trophy three consecutive times. He would win again in 1974 and 1980.

Every great career has ups and downs, and Trevino's nadir came in 1975, when he was actually struck by lightning at the Western Open. In 1976, Trevino underwent surgery for a herniated disc. The injury left his back weak and often prevented him from regular practice. But in 1984, at age forty-four, Trevino echoed his glorious past by shooting four straight rounds in the 60s and winning his second PGA title at Shoal Creek in Alabama. And he did it with a smile on his face. The hustler in Lee Trevino had carried him again.

(right) *He was always laughing and smiling and talking, but there was more to Lee Trevino than mere style. He was a top-flight golfer, who endured a number of hardships along the way—a humble beginning and a strike by lightning, to name a few. Trevino's great strength was his iron play (left). Like Walter Hagen before him, Trevino had a knack for salvaging some impossible predicaments. He always seemed to be at his best when it mattered most. In the 1988 Skins Game, he escaped with most of the cash by dropping a hole-in-one right in front of Jack Nicklaus and Arnold Palmer.*

Forget those six British Open titles. Focus on Harry Vardon's hands—those marvelous hands. It is the famous overlapping Vardon grip (right) that remains even today one of golfing's sacred fundamentals.

Harry Vardon

THERE ARE THOSE WHO MERELY PASS THROUGH GOLF and those, like Harry Vardon, who lend the sport a new luster. Along with James Braid and J.H. Taylor, Vardon formed the Great Triumvirate; together, between 1894 and 1914, they won sixteen British Open titles, placed second another twelve times, and so helped popularize golf in Great Britain.

Vardon himself won a never-equaled record of six Open championships, yet it was his unique approach to golfing that changed the game forever. Take, for instance, the widely acclaimed overlapping Vardon grip. It wasn't his creation alone, but he received most of the credit for its nearly universal acceptance.

He was born on May 9, 1870, in Grouville, Jersey, the fourth of six sons in a family of eight. By the time he was ten, Vardon was caddying at the course that would become the Royal Jersey Golf Club. Under the light of the moon, the boys would play the course themselves, using shafts cut from a black thorn tree, a club head whittled from oak, and a large white marble for the ball. At the time, club grips consisted of felt wrapped with leather and bound with twine. The broken clubs they came across had no grips and offered a thorny problem, so Vardon and his brother Tom made an adjustment. Golfers were already placing the little finger of their right hand over the index finger of the left and, quite often, their right thumbs down the shaft for

better stability, but the Vardons also placed the left thumb down the shaft, intergrating the hands. The result was a smoother, more sensitive swing — and hands that could grip the club more comfortably over a longer period.

And while most of his contemporaries were lunging at the ball on flat feet, Vardon was using a more upright swing that placed a premium on timing, rather than brute strength. Vardon eventually became the professional at Studley Royal and entered his first British Open in 1893, at age twenty-three. Three years later, Vardon won the title for the first time, beating Taylor by four strokes in a playoff at Muirfield, Scotland. Taylor had won the first two of his five Open championships in 1894 and 1895, and Vardon's victory signaled the emergence of a new rival.

Vardon won again in 1898 and 1899, at Prestwick, Scotland, and Royal St. George's in England. His fame had already spread to America when he visited there in 1900. Not only did he win the U.S. Open at Chicago Golf Club (edging Taylor), but Vardon's presence undoubtedly gave the game momentum. He was only too happy to demonstrate his swing and his grip in exhibition matches and clinics.

In 1913, after Vardon had amassed five British Open titles, he made another visit to America. There, a twenty-year-old amateur named Francis Ouimet beat him and countryman Ted Ray in a playoff that changed the game forever in the United States. A year later, at Prestwick, Vardon won his unprecedented sixth Open title. Even today, Americans understand his contribution to their golf game. When the Ryder Cup match is played in Britain, the American team has always made a point of visiting Vardon's grave at Totteridge Parish Church.

IN THE LATE 1970'S AND EARLY 1980'S, TOM WATSON WAS golf's dominant player. In a nine-year period between 1975 and 1983, Watson won eight major tournaments, including five British Opens.

As Jack Nicklaus settled into the final stages of his brilliant career, Watson seemed destined to take his place at the top of the game. In 1977, Watson won $310,653 to lead all players on the PGA Tour for the first time. Thus began Watson's amazing four-year reign as the leading money–winner and the Player of the Year. He took home $362,429 in 1978, $462,636 in 1979, and $530,808 in 1980. Watson was the first golfer to earn more than $500,000 in a season. In those four years, Watson won twenty-

one of the thirty-one tournaments he captured through the 1986 season.

Born in Kansas City, Missouri, on September 4, 1949, Watson was only six years old when his father, who hovered around par, first taught him the elements of the game. He went on to win the Missouri State Amateur title four times and played three years at Stanford University. In 1971, the year he graduated with a degree in psychology, Watson turned professional. His first start on the P.G.A. Tour, the Kaiser International Open, netted a tie for twenty-eighth place and a total of $1,065.

In 1975, Watson vaulted from 224th on the money list to seventy-ninth to thirty-fifth to tenth to seventh. That was the year

Tom Watson

he won his first major, the British Open at Carnoustie, Scotland. Watson tied with Jack Newton at 279, then beat him by a stroke with a 71 in the playoff. Two years later, Watson and chief adversary Jack Nicklaus would provide more dramatic theater. Earlier, at the Masters in Augusta, Watson had responded when Nicklaus came from three strokes down to fire a 66. He shot a 67 and won his first Masters title by two strokes. At Turnberry, Scotland, Watson and Nicklaus locked in a *mano a mano* duel that may never be equaled. The two heavyweights of the game shot identical rounds of 68–70–65 before Watson slipped past Nicklaus's 66 with a brilliant 65. Nicklaus holed out for a birdie on the last green and Watson answered with a birdie of his own.

Watson won the Masters a second time in 1981, defeating — who else? — Nicklaus and Johnny Miller with a 280 at Augusta. In 1982, he outplayed Nicklaus again in another marvelous tournament. It was the U.S. Open at Pebble Beach Golf Links in California and Nicklaus was already in the clubhouse with a 284. Technically, he was tied for the lead, but Watson's two-iron off the 209-year par-three No. 17 hole bounced into the heavy rough on the left side of the green. For years, Watson's sometimes errant drives had been the critics' explanation for Watson's U.S. Open drought, and now they probably chortled as he contemplated the possibility of a "million-in-one" shot. The ball, barely visible, seemed destined for a bogey. Then Watson chipped the ball into the cup for a birdie and bounced across the green, leaping for joy. His birdie at No. 18 was anticlimactic; Watson had defeated Nicklaus in the tournament he had never won yet wanted so badly.

© Bruce Mathews/Mathews Communications

Between 1977 and 1980, Tom Watson did an amazing thing: He led the PGA Tour in winnings for four straight years, collecting better than $1.6 million in the process. That kind of consistency has earned him six Player-of-the-Year honors, as well as five British Open titles.

Clearly buoyed, Watson crossed the Atlantic and won his fourth Masters title at Royal Troon in Scotland, then repeated again in 1983 at Royal Birkdale. Watson seemed on the verge of three straight Open triumphs and a tie with the great Harry Vardon's mark of six British Open championships. He and Seve Ballesteros were tied with two holes to play at St. Andrews, but the Spaniard closed with par-birdie to defeat Watson by two strokes. In any case, Watson equaled James Braid's accomplishment (1901 through 1910) of five Open titles in ten years.

In 1984, Watson was the PGA Tour's leading money-winner for the fifth time and named Player of the Year for the sixth time.

Kathy Whitworth did not burst on the golfing scene in the manner of Nancy Lopez or Jack Nicklaus. She began playing at the age of fifteen, won the New Mexico State Amateur championship in 1957 and 1958, then struggled for three years on the LPGA Tour. After that, there was no stopping her. In 1975, Whitworth was inducted into the Hall of Fame. Then, at an age when most athletes are thinking about retirement, Whitworth averaged two tournament victories and $100,000 a year for the next ten seasons.

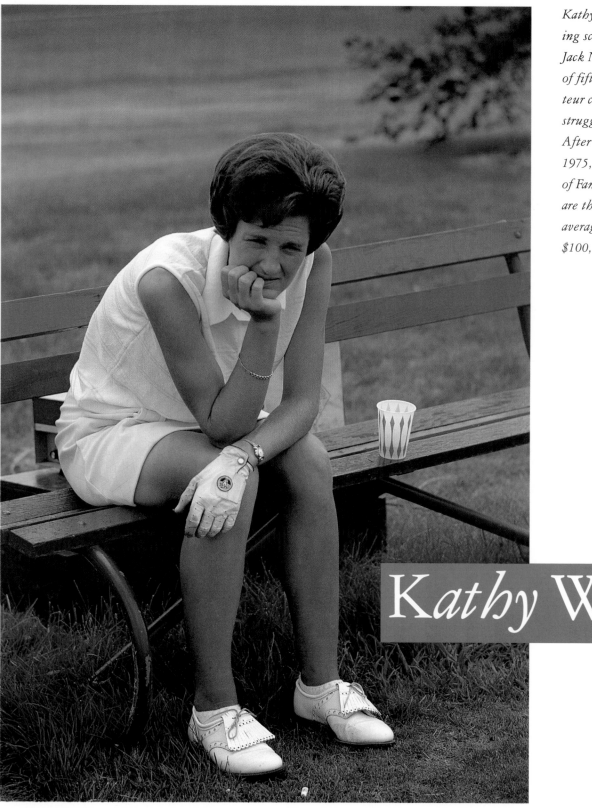

© Howard O. Allen

Kathy Whitworth

ON MARCH 20, 1983, KATHY WHITWORTH DROPPED A forty-foot putt on the seventy-second and final hole to win the Women's Kemper Open. That tied her with Sam Snead for the most official tournament victories by a professional in the United States. More than a year later, on July 22, 1984, Whitworth gained her eighty-fifth win at the Locust Hill Country Club's Rochester International to become the winningest golfer America had ever seen.

She is, without question, the standard against which all golfers on the LPGA Tour are judged. Whitworth was the first female golfer to reach the $1-million mark in earnings. Between the Fort Wayne Classic in 1959, when she took home $192.50 for a seventh-place finish, and the 1981 U.S. Women's Open, with its $9,000 payoff for third place, Whitworth has built an unparalleled career.

Witness this incredible run of dominance: over a period of nine years, from 1965 to 1973, Whitworth was the LPGA's leading money–winner eight times, the Player of the Year seven times, and the Vare Trophy winner (for best stroke average) another seven times. Even at the height of his game, Jack Nicklaus could not match Whitworth's sustained brilliance, the complete and utter command she had over her sport.

Born on September 27, 1939, in Monahans, Texas, Whitworth grew swiftly into a slim, 5-foot-9 athlete who started hitting golf balls at the age of fifteen. Under the tutelage of Harvey Penick and Hardy Loudermilk, Whitworth's skill became increasingly evident. She attended Odessa College and won the New Mexico State Amateur title in 1957 and 1958 before turning professional in December of 1958.

Golf lore is full of instant successes, but not in this case. Whitworth played in twenty-six tournaments in 1959 and won all of $1,217. Her best finish was a ninth and her stroke average was a rookielike 80.3. Two more years of scuffling led to Whitworth's first tournament victory, in 1962, at the Kelly Girl Open at the Turf Valley Country Club in Maryland. A win at the Phoenix Thunderbird Open soon followed. By 1963, Whitworth had forged herself into one of the game's best players. Initially in the shadow of Mickey Wright, up to that point the winningest women's golfer, Whitworth placed second to her in winnings that year and third in 1964. Whitworth led all players with a $28,658 season in 1965, moving ahead of Wright to stay. After that, it was a matter of catching all the marks Wright, four years Whitworth's senior, had set.

The victories came in a blur during the middle and late 1960s: Whitworth won eight tournaments in 1965, nine more in 1966, eight in 1967, and ten in 1968. She was enshrined in the LPGA Hall of Fame in 1975. Twenty years after her first tour victory,

Whitworth drew even with Wright by winning the 1982 C.P.C. International — her eighty-second success. A month later, Whitworth was the winner in the Lady Michelob at the Brookfield West Golf and Country Club. She had finally passed Wright.

Where does Whitworth now live? Appropriately, she now calls Trophy Club, Texas, home.

CHAMPIONS ARE RARELY PRODUCED BY ACCIDENT, AND Mickey Wright was no exception. She picked up her first golf club at the age of twelve in San Diego, and by age fourteen she already needed special attention. For two years, Wright and her mother drove 125 miles to San Gabriel every Saturday for a one hour lesson with Harry Pressler, the resident professional at San Gabriel Country Club.

Mickey Wright

Wright, born in San Diego on Valentine's Day in 1935, was a sturdy 5-foot-9 and could swing powerfully through the ball with her body. The results were dramatic. In 1952, at age seventeen, Wright won the U.S. Girls Junior championship. Her U.S. Open debut two years later was nearly as impressive. She was partnered with Babe Zaharias for the final day's double round and held her own as Zaharias completed her career in triumph. Wright finished in a tie for fourth and a torch of sorts had been passed. The experience convinced her to leave Stanford University and join the LPGA Tour in 1955.

There wasn't a golfer on the circuit who could hit it farther than Wright — accuracy, not distance, was the thing that often escaped her grasp, however. In that first year, Wright entered nineteen tournaments and once placed as high as third. Still, she needed seasoning. Wright's short game was appallingly weak and her control over her emotions usually fell into the same category. When she finally realized that she couldn't reach every green in two shots, Wright's chipping and putting became more polished. That made her very nearly unbeatable.

In 1958, Wright won the U.S. Open at Forest Lake Country Club in Michigan as well as the LPGA Championship at Churchill Valley Country Club in Pennsylvania. She won five tournaments in total that year and two years later began a spectacular run of victories. There were five that season, followed by ten each in 1961 and 1962, an incredible thirteen in 1963, and eleven in 1964. There were thirty-two LPGA tournaments in 1963 and Wright won forty percent of them. In both 1962 and 1963, Wright won four consecutive tournaments — something no one has ever come close to equaling. In nine years, Wright won seventy-nine of her eighty-two titles, averaging nearly eight victories a year.

Under pressure, there was no one better than Wright. Her thirteen majors are far and away the LPGA's record — Betsy Rawls is second with eight. Wright won the U.S. Open and

© Howard O. Allen

That picturesque swing (left) wasn't developed by accident, but was the product of an uncommon effort. Mickey Wright was literally driven to succeed in the game like no golfer before or after, and it is safe to say that no one in golf history dominated quite the way Wright did in 1963. That was the year she won 13 of 32 LPGA tournaments— better than 40 percent of the season's events.

© Kevin Vandivier/Viesti & Assoc. Inc.

LPGA Championship four times each. The LPGA record book is peppered with her accomplishments, including the best eighteen-hole score (62), which was shot at the Hogan Park Golf Club in Texas in 1964.

Wright went on to win those eighty-two tournaments, a figure bested only by Kathy Whitworth. Wright retired in 1970, but ten years later she pulled on a pair of sneakers and shot 70–74–72 to reach a five-way playoff in the Coca-Cola Classic. In 1985, she teamed with Whitworth in the PGA -sponsored Legends of Golf.

Undoubtedly, there might never have been a better female golfer than Mickey Wright.

The Best 18 Holes

ACCORDING TO THE 1987 PGA TOUR BOOK, THE PAR-THREE NO. 16 HOLE at Cypress Point is the most difficult hole on today's tour. In 1986, for instance, of the 178 professionals who teed off there in the A.T.&T. Pebble Beach National Pro-Am, only four managed birdie. There were 70 bogeys, 32 double-bogeys, and six unfortunate souls took triple-bogey. And as if that wasn't bad enough, the second-toughest hole PGA golfers face in the No. 17 hole at Cypress Point.

Those holes, of course, border on the ridiculous. Mortals shouldn't be forced to play them, but play them they do. The result is the agony of defeat and the thrill of anything approaching par. After man has conquered himself in the ongoing battle of nerves and self-doubt, there is always the course to consider. The following eighteen that have been selected could just as easily have been eighteen others, say the lovely par-four No. 18 at Muirfield, Scotland, or the testing par-four No. 15 hole at Westchester Country Club.

All of these holes have something in common. In addition to sharing an absorbing aesthetic quality, they demand that a golfer use his brains and, quite often, his imagination. Is that wind coming over the ridge leaving the hole a club longer? Or is it merely making a shot close to the flag impossible because of the green that slopes toward the lake guarding the front of the hole?

The best holes force the golfer to make a difficult decision. Once made, the choice must be properly executed. The reward is a chance for birdie. The penalty for a mistake can often amount to two or three strokes against par.

Take a tour here on eighteen holes that are as intellectually demanding as they are breathtaking to behold. From the gorgeous 155-yard, par-three No. 12 hole they call Golden Bell at Augusta National, to the monstrous 625-yard, par-five No. 16 at Firestone Country Club, experience the courses that make golf one of life's most complete sporting pleasures. But remember, bogey is par for this course.

Pebble Beach (left) *lies on gorgeous, pristine Carmel Bay in California. Yet golfing there can be anything but relaxing.*

No. 1: Hole 12 at AUGUSTA NATIONAL GOLF CLUB
Augusta, Georgia

The view at Augusta's No. 12 is spectacular. Yet golfers faced with the yawning Rae's Creek and those infamous bunkers don't usually take the time to enjoy the dogwood and azaleas that act as a backdrop to one of the world's most famous holes.

© Frank Christian

THE CHARMING NO. 12 HOLE AT AUGUSTA, PERHAPS THE greatest par-three in the world, was not a product of blueprints and bulldozers. It was lying hidden among the rolling hills of Georgia until Bobby Jones and architect Alister MacKenzie discovered it on the 365-acre site of a former horticulture nursery. The year was 1931, the Depression was raging, and money was tight, so the two builders built up the tee and planted a little grass around the green, which at one time served as an old Indian burial ground.

Today, the 155-yard hole at the apex of Amen Corner is the jewel of the Masters tournament. It is guarded zealously by Rae's Creek in front, three nasty bunkers, and a gentle hillside to the rear. When the wind blows, as it quite often does, the green can be very difficult to reach. Depending on the conditions — on the course and in your mind — anything from a three-iron to a seven-iron will do the job.

Here is what you face looking off the tee: The green is shaped like an hourglass lying on its side, with the right side pinched a little smaller. The pin is generally placed on the right side in competition because it forces a difficult club choice, and the two bunkers behind and one in front protect that side. There are roughly twenty feet to work with, which leaves less bold golfers firing for the fat part of the green to the left. Hit it short and risk losing your ball or landing in the front trap. Hit it long and you'll have to contend with the sloping hillside or those rear bunkers.

Many Masters have been won and lost at No. 12. In many ways, it is a make-or-break hole because it sets you up for the par-five No. 13 and No. 15 holes, which can be reached in two shots. In 1959, Arnold Palmer was defending his first Master's title and had a five-shot lead heading into No. 12. He landed in Rae's Creek and took a triple-bogey. Eventually, Art Wall birdied six of the last seven holes to win. Palmer finished third.

No. 2: Hole 4 at BALTUSROL GOLF CLUB Springfield, New Jersey

NOT ONLY IS THE PAR-THREE, 194-YARD NO. 4 HOLE AT Baltusrol's Lower Course one of golf's prettiest holes, it is also one of the most difficult — water, water everywhere, and bunkers beyond that. It is an oasis surrounded by trouble.

The original golf club here was built in 1895, at the dawn of golf history in America, and named for Baltus Roll, a farmer of Dutch extraction, who had been murdered on the land sixty years earlier. The course hosted two U.S. Opens, in 1903 and 1915, before it was ripped up and turned into two courses by golf architect A. W. Tillinghast. The No. 4 hole remains a favorite of the great players who have battled it.

It is almost a natural amphitheater, with its rising slope to the rear populated by dogwood and oak trees. There is a formidable lake guarding the front of the hole with a stone wall that faces the golfer as he tees off. The green is a large oval that slopes gently toward the lake with a two-level face that breaks diagonally across the middle. The back of the green is surrounded almost entirely by three bunkers and a fourth trap is placed in the front left corner, where the water ends. The creek that supplies the lake gobbles up any errant slices off the tee and there is heavy rough running around the edge of the green where the bunkers allow it.

In 1954, Robert Trent Jones did some remodeling of the course before the U.S. Open that was to be played there. Jones played the course one day with three Baltusrol administrators who suggested he had made the No. 4 hole too difficult, even for professionals. Jones smiled and watched his tee there clear the water and dive into the cup for hole-in-one.

Baltusrol is a tough enough course, but this vista from the No. 4 tee is enough to send the weak-kneed golfer back to the clubhouse. If the lake doesn't intimidate—the shifting wind makes club selection an adventure in itself—the four bunkers and the heavy rough might.

© Jim Moriarty

No. 3: Hole 17 at BAY HILL CLUB
Orlando, Florida

IMAGINE THIS UNHAPPY SIGHT AS YOU TEE UP YOUR BALL on the par-three No. 17 hole at Bay Hill: The flag is a distant speck, waving vaguely in the breeze some 233 yards away, and a long, narrow sand trap yawns along the entire front edge of the kidney-shaped green. The flag is in the middle of the green where it is most narrow, and there appears to be about three feet to shoot at, though there is really much more. If that isn't enough, there is a bunker to the left and a terrific trap kissing the back of the green, right along the line of your tee shot from its elevated position. And then there is the water. Yes, water. The hole requires a full carry over water, and if the wind is in your face, which it usually is, a long iron might not be enough, for it hardly offers the kind of control a delicate situation like this requires. It gets worse, too. There are alligators in the lake, and they like nothing better than to chew on duffers who top their balls into the water.

All of this deviousness can be blamed on the late Dick Wilson, who is acknowledged as one of golf's greatest architects. He had a wry sense of humor and a tremendous feel for the land he worked with. The No. 17 hole is one of his crowning efforts, since it brings all the elements of the game together by challenging a golfer's intellect as well as his physical talent. One of the nicest touches on the hole is the female scuba diver who retrieves balls that don't have enough steam on them.

In sum, the hole isn't terribly difficult if you manage to resist the temptation to shoot at the flag — just watch out for those alligators.

Thanks to golf architect Dick Wilson, the Bay Hill Club's par-three No. 17 hole is a challenge to both sides of the golfer's brain; he or she must size up the variable conditions, then hit the perfect shot.

No. 4: Hole 17 at CHERRY HILLS COUNTRY CLUB Denver, Colorado

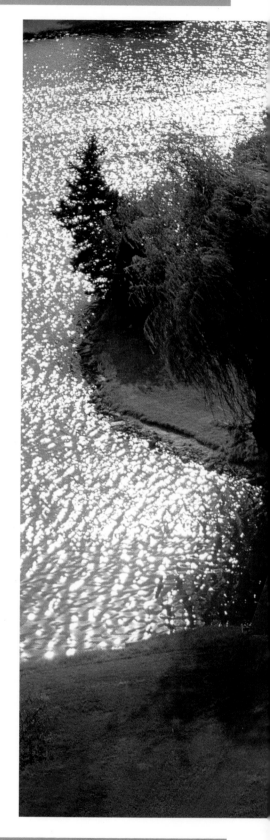

MOST PAR-FIVES ARE A TEST OF ENDURANCE. NOT SO THE 548-yard No. 17 hole at Cherry Hills — it's more like a fight for life. The highest possible premium is placed on accuracy. If the first perfect shot is not followed by a second, more exact stroke, you can forget about par. You can even forget about getting off the hole before dark.

On paper, the hole seems reachable with two shots. The catch is that the circular green is virtually an island; it is separated from the rest of the hole by a small creek that turns into a lake behind it. Only a small walkway makes this hole reachable by foot. The narrow fairway off the tee is lined by trees on both sides, so a long iron is highly recommended. The second shot must be hit with care — too strong a stroke leaves the ball in the water, too weak and you are facing an impossible wedge. So technically, the green can be reached in two shots. It's just that the odds of stopping a ball hit with a driver on that small green are remote indeed. Only the terribly brave, or foolish, attempt it.

Once safely on the unremarkable putting surface, getting down in two is a fairly easy matter. It's just the getting there that's difficult.

Cherry Hills is a championship course with a glorious history. Ralph Guldahl repeated his 1937 U.S. Open success at Oakland Hills Country Club in Michigan with a victory over Dick Metz at Cherry Hills. In 1941, Vic Ghezzi was one of the few people to beat Byron Nelson that year in the PGA at Cherry Hills. In 1960, Arnold Palmer won his first and only U.S. Open there in typically hard-charging fashion. He trailed by seven strokes on the final day, when he made six birdies on the first seven holes, then closed with a 66 to win by two strokes. In second place that year at Cherry Hills was a young amateur named Jack Nicklaus.

No man is an island, but there are times when the No. 17 at Cherry Hills can leave a golfer feeling awfully lonely. This aerial view of the circular green drives that point home, though players are advised here to eschew the unwieldy driver and hit long irons off the tee.

No. 5: Hole 17 at CYPRESS PT. CLUB *Pebble Beach, California*

CYPRESS POINT AT PEBBLE BEACH IS A MARVELOUS course by the ocean. The Pacific comes into play again and again on this splendid piece of the Monterey Peninsula, most dramatically on the No. 16 and No. 17 holes. The former, a par-three, is the most well known and requires a tee shot of some 233 yards over two inlets of rocky coastline. No. 17, however, is every bit as difficult. Alister MacKenzie, the cunning architect, planned it that way.

Just standing at the tee looking out toward the green as the 371-yard, par-four hole bends around the coastline to the right, can be enough to paralyze the most confident golfer — especially if he or she already has been humbled at No. 16. Like it or not, however, the shot must be made. Invariably the wind is in the golfer's face, which makes for a much longer hole. The roar of the sea, which the ball must travel across, doesn't help either. Even a driver might not be enough club to knock the ball far enough left to insure a clean line to the green. By marvelous design, a huge cypress tree is strategically located on the right side of the green precisely where it angles sharply to the right. Clearing that can be a chore in itself.

The green, perched on the edge of the ocean cliff, is shaped like a triangle with the base at the back, bordered by a large bunker. If, for some reason, the wind isn't gusting, the second shot can be relatively simple. On the other hand, if the breeze off Carmel Bay is kicking up, the ball — like the Scotch at the nineteenth hole — will be on the rocks.

Cypress Point, along with Pebble Beach and Spyglass Hill, used to be the site of the popular tournament hosted annually by Bing Crosby. At 6,317 yards, Cypress was by far the shortest. If the wind was tame, the tournament's low scores tended to come from Cypress. If not, it was strictly a battle of man against nature, especially on No. 17. Man rarely won.

Water, water everywhere, and not a . . . place large enough to safely land your second shot at No. 17 at Cypress Point Club. This kind of ocean view leaves the rocks as a less grim alternative—barely.

No. 6: Hole 18 at DORAL GOLF AND COUNTRY CLUB
Miami, Florida

Even when the flag is positioned in the tantalizing left-rear corner, the golfer at Doral's No. 18 hole is advised to keep his drive down the right side of the tilting fairway. Of course, a bunker is positioned there to keep par-seekers honest.

© Jim Moriarty

© Jim Moriarty

ON MANY COURSES, THE NO. 18 HOLE IS A CONCESSION to the spectators, a pretty picture postcard with the elegant clubhouse splashed across the background. The hole itself is often incidental. Not on the Blue Course at Doral. The 437-yard par-four is one of the most difficult finishing holes in golf.

To begin with, there is a lake that runs the length of the hole to the left; from tee to green, it never goes away. On the right are plenty of trees that come into play after a short tee shot. When pondering the drive, one must consider the lesser of the two evils and try to stay down the right side of the fairway. Why? The fairway is so severely angled that a shot hit anywhere along the left side will simply roll down into the lake. By going right, the golfer can also avoid a shot over a brief expanse of lake that dips

to the front left side of the hole. When the flag is placed in the back left, as it often is, flirting with the water can be fatal.

Depending on the wind, which is generally in the player's face and fairly strong toward the end of the day, anything from an eight-iron to a two-iron can be required for the second shot. The green may be nearly sixty yards deep, but with its radical slope the ball can disappear quickly. If you play it too safely to the right, the bunker will swallow the ball. A bogey is often the best one can hope for at Doral's No. 18.

The 6,939-yard course itself is not that difficult for the touring professionals. In 1986, for instance, seventy-two players made the one-under cut at 143. And every one of them was glad to complete the No. 18 and walk into the safety of the clubhouse.

No. 7: Hole 16 at FIRESTONE COUNTRY CLUB Akron, Ohio

The green at Firestone's No. 16 hole doesn't give in easily; a lake guards the front and a huge ditch lies to the right. From the tee, you can't see the forest for the trees.

Courtesy Firestone Country Club

THEY DON'T COME ANY TOUGHER THAN THIS ONE. FOR sheer brutality, the No. 16 on Firestone's South Course is unmatched. It is 625 arduous yards long and fraught with every danger imaginable on a golf course. The players have called it the Monster for years. It is a charitable name.

The tee shot on the hole that doglegs to the left must be kept to the left, for two formidable bunkers guard the right side, close to where most professional drives come to rest. Though they aren't particularly big, they are well placed on the very edge of the fairway, which slopes down toward the left. The perfect shot, then, must be hit as high as possible, yet miss the traps. Occasionally, the green can be reached in two shots. More often, it requires three, four, or five strokes to get there. The reason? The medium-sized green will not tolerate an error of more than a few feet.

There are trees down both sides of the fairway and the golfer does well to avoid those on the right. If the second shot lands anywhere to left of center, it will roll and roll into the rough or thick woods. Even a well-hit shot can lead to trouble, because there is a small lake that protects the front of the green, leaving only a tiny opening on the left side. There is also a deep ditch thoughtfully tucked just short of the lake and to the right. Naturally, the pin is usually placed in the right front section of the green. Most professional golfers try to hit a pair of accurate three-woods and reach the green with a seven– or eight–iron.

There are two more water hazards around the hole, small troughs to the right of the green and behind it. Two bunkers keep the green's left flank covered. There are trees everywhere. Once on the green safely, the golfer is rewarded with reasonable conditions. By that time, however, it is usually too late.

Courtesy Firestone Country Club

No. 8: Hole 16 at HAZELTINE NATIONAL GOLF CLUB *Chaska, Minnesota*

GOLFERS HAVE NEVER BEEN THE MOST ROUGH-HEWN LOT. Cheering is generally frowned on when the athletes are executing their strokes. The golfing psyche is a fragile one, especially if the course seems to be getting the better of the play. Nowhere was this delicate situation better illustrated than at Hazeltine in the 1970 U.S. Open.

Frankly, the U.S.G.A. officials sometimes get a little too excited when they prepare U.S. Open courses — they let the rough grow a little too deep and carve out some beastly pin placements. The courses are usually long and tight and unforgiving. "They ought to plow it up and start all over again," said Dave Hill after a seventy-two-hole tour of the Hazeltine course. Of course, Hill's rancor might have been tied to his second-place finish to British hero Tony Jacklin. Just maybe. Certainly, the Robert Trent Jones layout was testing, and there were some truly dreadful holes — but plow it up and start over?

Perhaps the most imaginative hole is the No. 16, which is a par-three that plays 214 yards long. No. 16 is a self-contained dogleg: When the flag is set off to the far left side of the green, it can't be seen from the tee. The swaying trees simply won't allow it. On the right side, the trees are a welcome addition to the hole, since Lake Hazeltine awaits the unlucky golfer who manages to leave his tee shot out to the right.

Even under optimum conditions, No. 16 is a difficult par proposition. But when the winds begin swirling, changing direction with every passing moment, the real fun begins. Club selection varies widely, and once on the green, a hump in the middle can make getting down in two an adventure. It was a great adventure for Tony Jacklin during the 1970 U.S. open — he only three-putted once and played it in a reasonable one over par.

It may look serene and bucolic, but do not be fooled: The sixteenth at Hazeltine is treacherous.

No. 9: Hole 2 at MEDINAH COUNTRY CLUB Medinah, Illinois

SOME HOLES, LIKE THE NO. 2 HOLE AT MEDINAH'S NO. 3 course, aren't meant to be birdied. The professional is wise to play for par at this 184-yard par-three, otherwise he may find himself all wet — both literally and figuratively.

This gem doesn't enjoy the marquee value placed on the No. 12 hole at Augusta National or the ocean-edged finishing hole at Pebble Beach. Arnold Palmer never charged past a failing field here; Jack Nicklaus didn't outduel Tom Watson on this storied course. The players on the PGA tour do not have a pet name for it. When you are a No. 2 hole, you don't get much respect; most of golf's theatrics occur late in a round. When the day is over, not many people can remember all the way back to the No. 2 hole. Too bad.

As the golfer contemplates his tee shot, the first thing that attracts attention is the water stretching completely across his path to the distant green. To the right of the rectangular-shaped putting surface is a small bunker that doesn't come into play too often. That is because the pinsetters like to place the flag in the worst possible spot — the front left corner, where a kidney-shaped bunker protects the left side and the water laps only a few feet from the fringe in front of the green. Past the sand trap to the left is more water still. There are trees scattered just about everywhere else and a road that runs behind the hole if the water intimidates the golfer into hitting too strong a shot.

The only rule here is to avoid shooting at the stick — the price of an automatic double-bogey is too great. Most players aim for the middle of the green with a five, six, or seven-iron and take their chances with two putts. A ball that seems perfectly placed can actually land near the pin and, with too much backspin, roll right off the fast, sloping green into the water.

On the surface, 184 yards doesn't seem to be an insurmountable obstacle for a two-shot birdie. Wrong. Though it doesn't get proper credit, the No. 2 hole at Medinah is one of golf's more demanding venues.

No. 10: Hole 13 at MERION GOLF CLUB Ardmore, Pennsylvania

ALTHOUGH MOST TRULY CHAMPIONSHIP COURSES ARE close to 7,000 yards long, Merion's East Course is a notable exception. Touch and feel are often as important as raw power on this classic layout. Like the course itself, the No. 13 hole is deceptively short. Its magnificent construction, however, leaves a golfer thinking the 129-yard par-three is twice as long.

Unlike many of the great par-threes, the No. 13 at Merion does not introduce water hazards into the difficult equation. But the five sprawling bunkers that seem to surround the oval green actually occupy more space than the putting surface itself. It's no wonder golfers are forever dropping into them. When the pin is placed at the front in championship events, golfers who want to get close for a potential birdie run the risk of landing in the large trap that runs along the right-front fringe of the green. The edge of the trap runs just under that fringe and extraction can be nearly impossible. And that's if you can manage a decent lie. Merion's picturesque bunkers are laced with tall outgrowths of grass and there are at least a dozen menacing clumps around the green at No. 13. Most professionals just hope the ball lands somewhere, anywhere, on the green.

The Merion Cricket Club was founded in 1865, but the East Course wasn't built for another forty-five years. Cricket and tennis held court until golf gradually gained popularity. Some of the game's greatest moments came at Merion. In 1916, Bobby Jones played in his first U.S. Amateur at Merion, at the age of fourteen. Fourteen years later he defeated Eugene Homans in the U.S. Amateur final to cap his celebrated Grand Slam. It was here that Ben Hogan won the 1950 U.S. Open in a triumphant return from near-tragedy. Dragging his mangled legs around the course for four rounds wasn't enough — he was forced to a playoff with Lloyd Mangrum and George Fazio. Hogan fired a brilliant 69 and won. And in 1960, a twenty-year-old amateur named Jack Nicklaus stunned the golf world with a 66-67-68-68 to lead the United States to its first win in the world amateur championship and the Eisenhower Trophy.

Just outside of Philadelphia, you'll find bunkers that look like something from Scotland's finest courses. The No. 13 hole at Merion's East Course is protected by a sand trap laced with tall outgrowths of grass.

No. 11: Hole 15 at OAKMONT COUNTRY CLUB
Oakmont, Pennsylvania

© Jim Moriarty

*There are no gimmicks here: As this aerial
view shows (right),* the No. 15 hole at Oakmont is long on length and sand.

OAKMONT BEATS GOLFERS THE OLD FASHIONED WAY.
There are no water hazards at all, very few trees in play. There is,
however, plenty of sand and length, and then more sand and
more length. The U.S.G.A. likes this sort of approach, which
explains why a record six U.S. Opens have been staged here.

The No. 15 hole best typifies what W.C. Fownes had in mind
when he built the storied course in 1903. Over the years, the hole
that Ben Hogan once called the most demanding he had ever
played has lost a few of its teeth. When Hogan won the 1953 U.S.
Open here by edging Sam Snead, players didn't have the state-
of-the-art equipment available today; the 453-yard, par-four hole
was scaled perfectly for yesterday's game. There are bunkers to
the right and left of the spot where tee shots once came to rest,
though now they don't enter play as often. Still, this hole has its
considerable moments.

For starters, the flag isn't visible from the tee. The hulking
group of trees ahead and to the right of the tee, combined with
the hole's gentle dogleg to the right, make sighting the hole
impossible. Nonetheless, only a stout shot to the left-hand side
of the fairway is safe, because the slope from left to right will
carry anything less into the bunker or nearby drainage ditch.
That's the easiest part. The green, nearly 200 feet long from front
to back, seems to be an inviting target. The first sixty feet of the
putting surface slope away from the player, followed by a
gradual leveling off toward the rear. The small valley across the
front half of the green demands a delicate pitch-and-run if the
flat is forward. Any ball that lands toward the back of the green is
considered an automatic bogey — you can't get there in two
from here.

The bunkers around the green are troublesome. The narrow
furrow on the right side of the hole is as long as a football field
and well placed on the edge of the woods. Another long trap
protects the left side of the green. The way the green is
constructed, hitting that bunker might be the cautious golfer's
best bet.

Courtesy Oakmont Country Club

No. 12: Hole 16 at OLYMPIC CLUB
San Francisco, California

HERE IS A HOLE WITH A HISTORY THAT MATCHES ITS ability to frustrate even the best golfers. The 604-yard, par-five No. 16 hole on Olympic's Lake Course has been the scene of some of the game's greatest swings of emotion. Ben Hogan, in pursuit of an unprecedented fifth U.S. Open title in 1955, ran into difficulty here and wound up losing to an unknown golfer named Jack Fleck in a playoff. Fleck saved par at No. 16 in memorable fashion after finding the rough. Arnold Palmer had a seven-shot lead with nine holes to play in the last regulation round of the 1966 U.S. Open and the No. 16 hole played a pivotal role. He hooked his drive into the heavy rough and eventually took bogey. Billy Casper birdied the hole, forcing a playoff, and then beat Palmer by four strokes.

This is the longest of Olympic's holes and it gently curves around to the left. The fairway from tee to green is exceedingly narrow, and, as Palmer discovered in 1966, the rough can be rough. The first shot, a drive or three-wood, should be played to the right, and the second demands a similar method. The hole's distance forces a golfer to constantly flirt with danger: If the ball isn't hit with sufficient club, a long iron will be necessary to reach the green in three, and that means potential bunker trouble. Of course, there isn't much margin for error in that tight fairway. This is the kind of intellectual challenge that sends purists into ecstacy — or a delirious rage.

A tree stands short of the green to its left and should be studiously avoided. Generally, a six-or seven-iron will deliver the ball to the long oval green. The hole's major hazard is a good-sized bunker to the right of the green. A smaller trap covers the left front corner. There is a fair fringe around the back, but trees are clustered just behind it. Most professionals consider themselves lucky to par — certainly Hogan and Palmer would have been only too happy to accept a five here.

A long and narrow fairway awaits golfers on the par-five, 604-yard sixteenth hole at the Olympic Club in San Francisco.

No. 13: Hole 8 at PEBBLE BEACH GOLF LINKS
Pebble Beach, California

The No. 8 hole at Pebble Beach can play like a lamb if the volatile weather cooperates. If not, relax, aim for the bunker, and take a bogey-five.

© Dodo's Photos

THERE IS SOMETHING ABOUT THE SEA THAT INSPIRES AWE. This is the feeling one experiences at the tee of the No. 7 hole at Pebble Beach. For the next four holes, it is a constant struggle between man and his environment. Guess who prevails more often?

Like the Cypress Point Club that sits similarly on the Monterey Peninsula just a few miles away, Pebble Beach runs alongside gorgeous Carmel Bay. It is the happy meeting of land and sea here that makes Pebble Beach so memorable. The No. 7 hole is a 110-yard par-three with a small green crammed among the rocks; the No. 9 and No. 10 holes are long, sturdy par-fours with fairways that lean toward the water. The No. 8 hole is pure heaven — unless you happen to be playing it.

The hole bends around rather severely to the right, and the golfer will do well to stop his blind tee shot short of the jagged rocks that dominate the yawning chasm that sits inside the elbow. The fairway takes a more sedate route, twisting toward

the hole; it's important to remember that the shortest distance between two points, after all, is a straight line. As always with a links course, the weather dominates club selection. With the wind at your back, a long iron is needed to keep the tee shot from running on the rocks and the second shot from blowing past the green and into a bunker. If the wind is blowing in, even a pair of woods won't guarantee a place on the green. The second shot, if hit properly, sails across the stunning piece of scenery toward the heavily trapped green.

There are two traps in front of the green and another huge bunker that runs alongside the hole to the right. Considering the salty alternative a little farther right, the trap isn't such a bad place to be. The safe shot, of course, is a second shot to the fairway just short of the green and a short wedge to within one-putt range. Easier said than done. The No. 18 hole gets most of the publicity at Pebble Beach, but it doesn't offer the mental challenge of No. 8 on a good, windy day.

No. 14: Hole 2 at PINE VALLEY
Clementon, New Jersey

PINE VALLEY HAS BEEN DESCRIBED AS THE WORLD'S toughest inland course, and, according to the professionals there, the No. 2 hole plays tougher than any other. And that is saying something.

To begin with, the 367-yard, par-four is a narrow driving hole. At its maximum width, the fairway measures 45 yards across. There are a series of dangerous church-pew bunkers to the right side and a number of pot bunkers on the left. The green, a surface that is elevated some forty feet above the tee, is not easily gained. A vast waste area dominates the area between the bunkers and the fairway. If your ball lands there, write the hole off as a double or triple–bogey. This unkempt mess of a hazard is the essence of Pine Valley — the pristine modern courses wouldn't dream of troubling their patrons with such deviousness. The green itself slopes toward the tee, and two pot bunkers face it. It also features two swells, while three high ridges run the length of the green, from back to front. Three-putting is considered good form here.

The 184-acre layout is a unique piece of work. It was conceived by Philadelphia hotelman George Crump and H. S. Colt, a well-known course designer, and required seven years to build. According to records, more than 20,000 pine trees were uprooted to carve out the course, which is an amazing tangle of sand, scrub, and, every so often, emerald grass. Pine Valley is rarely acknowledged by the casual golf fan, but purists from Ben Crenshaw to Jack Nicklaus sing its praises. Pine Valley hosted the Walker Cup matches in 1936, and then again in 1985. There will never be a major tournament there; the course's dense natural hazards make it impossible to accommodate spectators. But golfers who are fortunate enough to tee it up at Pine Valley and survive eighteen holes know they have played one of the world's finest.

Now, here is something completely different: Pine Valley is an inland golf course that offers all the difficulty of the links layouts in Scotland. The No. 2 hole is particularly rough; there's a monstrous waste area that makes the pot bunkers seem like child's play.

No. 15: Hole 17 at
ST. ANDREWS
Fife, Scotland

TO STEP ONTO THE 6,960-YARD LAYOUT AT THE ROYAL and Ancient Golf Club's Old Course at St. Andrews is to step back into a different era, a time when golf was a gentleman's game. The club's records go all the way back to 1754, when the game was in its infancy. Tom Kidd won the first British Open played at St. Andrews, in 1873, and Seve Ballesteros won the most recent Open contested there, in 1984. In the intervening 111 years, aside from a few small alterations, not much has changed.

Technically, the course was never built. It was already there 500 years ago. Some theorize that the famous bunkers that dot the course began as protective shelters for the sheep who grazed there. Around the beginning of the nineteenth century, the course included twenty-two holes, as was in fashion then. After playing the first (and only) eleven holes, one turned around and played them in the opposite direction. By 1830, it had evolved into nine holes, with different pin placements for the back nine. Today, only four holes — the No. 1, No. 9, No. 17, and No. 18 — have their own green. St. Andrews' vast, double greens are the club's most obvious trademark. Most of them are studies in topography, with swirls and peaks and undulations that can leave even the best professional golfer embarrassingly far from his target. And that disagreeable fate is reserved only for those who survive the harrowing bunkers.

The bunkers have some lovely names that truly capture their essence: Hell Bunker, Grave Bunker, Cat's Trap, and so on. The holes all have names, too; the most famous is undoubtedly the No. 17 Road Hole. It is a 461-yard, par-four bit of treachery that has brought some of the greatest golfers to their knees. The bunkers here are difficult to see until your ball has found them: Cheape's Bunker, Scholar's Bunker, Progressing Bunker, and, of course, Road Bunker.

The Road Bunker, naturally, is the thrust of this endeavor. The No. 17 hole is laid out along the outside of the course as it closes toward the hotel and clubhouse. If your second shot strays to the right, you have no choice — you must cross the Road Bunker to see if your ball is on the other side. This happened to Tom Watson in 1984. In the final round of the British Open, Watson bounced his second shot over the Road Bunker and up against the old stone wall that separates the huge gallery from the hole. He bogeyed while Ballesteros parred, failing in his bid to win three straight titles and tie Harry Vardon's record of six overall.

Part of the charm at St. Andrews is the stunning view at the No. 17 hole. In 1984, Tom Watson did not find it appealing at all—his ball strayed to the right and he lost a chance for three consecutive triumphs in the British Open.

© Jack Foley/ENVISION

No. 16: Hole 17 at TOURNAMENT PLAYERS CLUB
Ponte Vedra Beach, Florida

FOR SHEER, STUNNING AUDACITY, THERE IS NO HOLE better than the seventeenth at the TPC at Sawgrass in Ponte Vedra Beach. No man is an island, but this hole surely is.

The 132-yard, par-three challenge sits alone in a lake, with only a narrow causeway permitting access. Very simply, this hole requires an all-or-nothing effort. The medium-sized green has a narrow fringe all the way around it and even a small bunker on the right front corner. It has moved men to tears and more than a few fears. Recently, a national golfing magazine collected some of the world's worst amateur golfers and allowed them to play the TPC at Sawgrass club. One of them began stroking the ball with his putter along the walkway, down the causeway and onto the green. In all, he required 47 shots.

The No. 17 hole is a microcosm for the entire course. Construction began in early 1979 and PGA Tour commissioner Deane Beman wanted it to be both an eyeful and a challenging course, mostly because it was the showcase for the Players Championship. He got his wish. The 6,857-yard layout is built on forty acres, or roughly half the space required of most courses. Golf architect Pete Dye wove a course in and around the natural sandy wastelands and immediately created a controversy. It was the first of the world's stadium courses, built with the goal of providing spectators with sweeping vantage points. Today, there are more courses based on Dye's careful sculpting.

The professionals, however, could do without the course. It offended, they said, their sense of fair play, and they complain that the vast stretches of sand claim more than their share of errant balls. (PGA officials point out that the greens have since been changed, thus players now enjoy the course.) On many holes, water is a factor. On No. 17 at Ponte Vedra Beach, it is the only factor.

© Bill Knight/Pro Photo Inc.

© Bill Knight/Pro Photo Inc.

The No. 17 hole at the Tournament Players Club at Sawgrass in Ponte Vedra Beach, Florida, combines a touch of Hollywood and a touch of madness. There is absolutely no margin for error when aiming for this green. An island paradise, it's not.

No. 17: Hole 9 at TURNBERRY Ayrshire, Scotland

THERE IS NO MORE BEAUTIFUL HOLE IN GOLF THAN THE No. 9 at Turnberry's Ailsa Course. Period. The stunning white lighthouse sits on a pile of rock, hard by the Firth of Clyde; in the distance, the familiar outline of the Mull of Kintyre can be seen along the horizon. Nearby resides Ailsa Craig, the landmark stone that rises out of the ocean.

And to think that it all might have been destroyed by the ravages of war. During World War II, the Royal Air Force constructed runways across the land for its Coastal Command. The site was considered strategic, considering its proximity to the sea, and thus coal-black tarmacs quickly replaced green fairways. When tensions finally relaxed, Scottish architect Mackenzie Ross was charged with rebuilding Turnberry. Rarely do such makeovers exceed the original version, but Ross stroked an eagle when he unveiled the course in time for the 1977 British Open. It was one of the most memorable Open contests in the event's history, which reaches all the way back to 1860, when Willie Park edged Tom Morris, Sr., with a 174.

In 1977, Jack Nicklaus and Tom Watson seemed to inspire each other, or maybe it was simply the beauty of their surroundings. How could they have been unmoved by the natural splendor as they tore through the field? Both men matched each other stroke for stroke, 68–70–65, before Watson won with a 65 on Sunday, compared to Nicklaus's 66.

The 455-yard, par-four No. 9 hole was as good a way to frame their remarkable achievement as any other. The hole is called Bruce's Castle, and it begins with a view fit for any self-respecting monarch. The tee is delicately balanced on an outcrop of rocks. The golfer's first shot — if indeed he can convince himself to take it — must carry over a series of wicked rocks to reach the narrow fairway, which runs on a high ridge. After that, the hole is almost anticlimactic. Getting home in four strokes is impressive, but it never quite approaches the scenery.

An ancient lighthouse watches over the No. 9 hole at Turnberry, a course that survived World War II in triumphant fashion.

No. 18: Hole 10 at WINGED FOOT GOLF CLUB
Mamaroneck, New York

One of the reasons Winged Foot grudgingly accepts below-par scores is the problematic No. 10 hole. The two traps fronting the green discourage a safe, short shot, but an iron over the green will flirt with the out-of-bounds markers.

© Leonard Kamsler

U.S. OPEN COURSES ARE CHOSEN WITH CARE. DEGREE OF difficulty is the overriding concern, and over the years Winged Foot's West Course has delivered consistently. It wasn't until the fourth U.S. Open was played there, in 1984, that someone finally broke par. (Fuzzy Zoeller and Greg Norman tied at four-under-par 276 before Zoeller won the playoff by eight strokes with a 67.) In 1974, Hale Irwin got around the fabled circuit in 287 and somehow managed to beat Forrest Fezler by two strokes.

Blame A. W. Tillinghast, who designed the course in 1923. Clearly, he had a perverse sense of humor, which is evident on the 180-yard, par-three No. 10 hole. The idea is to reach the medium-sized green that pinches in front and rises toward the back and avoid the danger that lurks all around it — no easy task. The favored club here is the three-iron, and the golfer must sneak over two sand traps that stretch across the front of the green. There is only a small opening between them, so hitting short can be a disaster. Long is not an option, either. Less than twenty feet behind the hole loom the out-of-bounds stakes. The trap on the left is the lesser of two evils, when the steep slope that takes a ball clear down to the trees is considered.

The green, scored with gentle undulations, is more difficult when the pin is set in the back. The uphill putt for birdie is usually fruitless. If the flag is up front and the golfer manages to steer clear of the fronting bunkers, there is a chance for a two.

The No. 10 hole is a pleasant intellectual challenge, a brief respite before Winged Foot's closing five holes — long par-fours all. They range from the 417-yard No. 15 to the 452-yard No. 16 and have contributed to the high numbers over time.

© Jim Moriarty

The *Professional Golfer's Association*

THE PROFESSIONAL GOLFER'S ASSOCIATION WAS NOT A HIGHLY organized, well-oiled corporate machine in its early days. Back in the 1920s, the best of the club professionals would peer out at the snow around their respective eighteenth holes and head south. They migrated to places like Florida and Texas, where the golf associations would hold regional and national events. Slowly, the professionals worked their way back toward home and their clubs in time to open the season at home.

It wasn't long before the larger hotels and resorts began to understand the important relationship between golf and commerce. Bobby Jones and Walter Hagen could play golf, of course, but they could also bring people in the front door. The number of tournaments grew and so did the purses. The Great Depression put a crimp in those fast times, but by 1934 the PGA had begun keeping records. History tells us that one Paul Runyan, who won six tournaments, was the leading money-winner that year — he took home $6,767.

Though the Tour became more stable through the 1940s as talents like Sam Snead, Byron Nelson, and Ben Hogan began to dominate, it hadn't yet captured the American marketplace. Then, in the late 1950s, Arnold Palmer blazed out of Latrobe, Pennsylvania, and carried golf to new heights. Here was an athlete. He didn't wear plus fours or a bow tie; he didn't quite fit the genteel image that golf had so long sought to establish. No, Arnie attacked the golf course and that was exciting. Golf...exciting?

Tom Watson (left) *is one of the brightest stars on the PGA Tour today.*

© Jim Moriarty

© Joe McNally/Wheeler Pictures

Television, that great instrument of exposure, was the other catalyst. The combination was irresistible. In 1958, Palmer was the Tour's leading money winner, with $42,607. Five years later, in the landmark 1963 season, Palmer won seven tournaments and took home $128,230. He was the first golfer to achieve that plateau, paving the way for all the glory and gold that followed. That was Palmer's last year on top. He gave way to Jack Nicklaus and Tom Watson, who pushed golf into the major leagues of American sport.

On January 25, 1970, Nicklaus won his first million with a second-place finish in the Bing Crosby — this eight years after he had taken home his first professional check, for $33.33, in the Western Open. Nicklaus hit $2 million less than four years later,

© Bill Knight/Pro Photo Inc.

in 1973, $3 million in 1977, $4 million in 1983, and $5 million in 1987. Watson, only thirty-eight, is already working on his fifth million.

In 1938, the PGA sponsored 38 tournaments and offered a total of $158,000 in prizes. In 1987, there were 46 events and an amazing total purse of $25,442,242. Since Palmer first cleared the $100,000 mark, the Tour's purses have multiplied more than ten times over. For eleven months of the year, golf is being played for big stakes every weekend somewhere in America. Through the winter months, the Tour whets the appetite of those who can't imagine golf greens under snowdrifts. In early January, the professionals first tee it up in Carlsbad, California, for the MONY Tournament of Champions. Bob Hope hosts a

Jack Nicklaus (above) *has won over $5 million on the PGA Tour to date; Severiano Ballesteros* (center) *and Greg Norman* (left) *continually are among golf's top performers also.*

tournament played over three courses in California, followed by contests played on the familiar venues of the Waialae Country Club (Hawaiian Open), the Riviera Country Club (Los Angeles Open), the Doral Country Club (Doral Ryder Open) in Miami, and the TPC at Sawgrass (The Players Championship) in Ponte Vedra, Florida. In April, the Masters holds forth at Augusta National, and two months later the U.S. Open is played on one of the nation's more tortuous courses — short on fairway and long on rough. The PGA Championship is the highlight of the August calender, then the professionals play through the middle of December, winding up again by design on the lush courses in Florida and California.

Always, money talks. There are some fairly amazing corporate and celebrity marriages that produce tournament names like the Canon Sammy Davis, Jr., Greater Hartford Open, and the Shearson Lehman Brothers Andy Williams Open. Don't forget about the Walt Disney World/Oldsmobile Golf Classic, either.

In recent years, the PGA Tour has become global in scope. For instance, there are now official tours in Europe, Japan, and Australia/New Zealand. All are terribly lucrative. Greg Norman took home $839,341 from the Australian Tour, while Tommy Nakajima ($773,497) and Bernhard Langer ($512,481) were the leading money-winners in Japan and Europe. Bob Tway, the U.S. PGA leader, won a relatively disappointing $720,574, if that kind of money can be viewed as disappointing.

Despite what people might think, this is hardly easy money. The PGA Tour has strict rules about who plays on the circuit. The first 125 players on the previous year's money list are automatically exempt from the difficult process of qualifying before each tournament. So are the winners of the PGA Championship and U.S. Open prior to 1970, and victors in PGA events within a two-year calendar period. Every year, the PGA develops its own talent in the PGA Qualifying Tournament. The first 50 finishers are exempt for the following year. Those who don't qualify for exemptions are reduced to "rabbit" status. They travel the tour in tired sedans and try to gain entrance to each field with early-morning rounds whose spectators can be counted on one hand.

Mac O'Grady was an unlucky rabbit for years. (He was born Phil McGleno, but in 1978 changed his name. At first, it didn't change his luck.) He tried Qualifying School in October of 1971 and failed miserably. He would try again sixteen more times before he finally made it in 1982 — a total he considers a PGA record. O'Grady is now one of the best golfers on the Tour and in 1986 won the tournament in Hartford, Connecticut. "It could only have happened on the PGA Tour," O'Grady says.

Today's PGA Tour is a highly organized, well publicized series of contests that inevitably draw large crowds.

The Ladies Professional Golf Association

THINK ABOUT THIS FOR A MOMENT: WHICH WOMEN'S SPORT HAS ONE OF the largest and most efficient organizations sanctioning and overseeing its competitive events? Golf. Though tennis doubtless generates more support worldwide, it is golf's example that future enterprises will borrow from.

The Ladies Professional Golf Association gained credibility in a male-dominated arena slowly and steadily through the 1960s and 1970s. It is no mere coincidence that the women's liberation movement traced a parallel course in society.

According to historical documents, there were women playing golf as far back as the 1840s. The wives of fishermen in Musselburgh, Scotland, tried their hand at the game, and by 1868 the Westward Ho! and North Devon Ladies Club had been formed. The competition was somewhat restrained by today's standards — play took place only on alternate Saturdays and women were restricted to a single club, the putter. Ladies, after all, did not take a vicious full swing at the ball. In 1893, Issette Pearson established the Ladies Golf Union. The British Women's Amateur championship soon followed, and Cecil Leitch and Joyce Wethered won four titles each in 1914 and 1929.

In America, the idea of a women's tour first took hold in 1944. Three obscure golfers named Betty Hicks, Hope Seignious, and Ellen Griffin established the Women's Professional Golf Association. For five years the W.P.G.A. struggled along with no particular direction, disappearing in 1948 and being replaced by the

Two of the LPGA's greatest together again: Mickey Wright (left) and Kathy Whitworth (right).

The LPGA has had its share of superstars and media sensations, including Patty Berg (left), the first inductee into the LPGA Hall of Fame; Carol Mann (right), and JoAnne *Carner (far right).*

© Howard O. Allen

LPGA. Fred Corcoran, the personal manager of Babe Didrikson Zaharias, became the marketing director for the new organization. At the time, Zaharias was a worldwide sensation, and Corcoran was determined to take advantage of the platform she provided. He raised $45,000 for nine tournaments in 1950, and, predictably, Zaharias won six of them. Patty Berg, the first president of the LPGA and one of its founders, won two titles that year.

Berg took up the game at the age of twelve, and three years later had already won the Minneapolis City Championship. Over the next seven years, Berg would win a total of twenty-nine tournaments as an amateur. She turned professional in 1940 and would win fifty-five tournaments before she stopped playing competitively, in 1980, at age sixty-two. During the mid 1950s, Berg dominated the Tour as the leading money-winner three times and amassed most of her fifteen major titles. She was the first golfer inducted into the LPGA Hall of Fame.

During the first two years of LPGA play, Zaharias and Berg won nineteen of twenty-three tournaments. Soon, the money and new respectability were enough to begin coaxing some of the good amateurs into the professional ranks — some. Like football in its early stages, women's professional golf was seen as something less than a proper sport. "You couldn't make money doing it," says Betsy Rawls, the Tour's leading winner in 1952 with six titles. "We practically had to beg people to turn professional. If you played golf then, you really loved the game."

Total purses crept ahead from that original $45,000 to more than $200,000 in 1959. In 1961, Mickey Wright was the LPGA's leading money-winner for the first of four times and the game continued to grow with her. Wright's exploits — she won forty-five tournaments, including four consecutively — drew the attention of the media. Television first trained its cameras on the LPGA in 1963, when the final round of the U.S. Open at Kenwood Country Club in Cincinnati was broadcast nationally. This offered the women's golf movement a new window to America. And the people liked what they saw.

Kathy Whitworth, Carol Mann, Jane Blalock, and JoAnne Carner gave the LPGA a new competitive depth. The total purse in 1973 amounted to $1.5 million. And then, temporarily, the bottom fell out. The burgeoning empire, moving too far too fast, found itself on the verge of bankruptcy in the mid-1970s. Enter Ray Volpe, a former National Hockey League marketing whiz. He became the first LPGA Commissioner and immediately fixed his attention on the organization's goals. Instructively, his first major step was to move the LPGA headquarters from Atlanta to New York City. That is corporate America's business address, and Volpe understood that the future of women's golf was tied to sponsorship.

In seven years with the LPGA Volpe watched the total purse rise from $1.5 million to $6.4 million, which breaks down to a rise from $50,000 to $176,000 per tournament. Suddenly, as many as fourteen tournaments were on television, instead of only two. Today, the LPGA is an organization bristling with confidence. The new headquarters, at Sweetwater Country Club in Sugar Land, Texas, is evidence of the LPGA's new independence.

Not that marketing has been forgotten. The LPGA is keenly aware that pretty faces don't hurt their cause. Makeup, in many cases, is just part of the equipment. Witness Australian Jan Stephenson, the sex symbol of the Tour. She is a slim 5-foot-5, with stunning blonde hair and blue eyes. She and other LPGA luminaries have posed provocatively for the cameras, giving the tour, uh, tremendous exposure. That Stephenson can play golf — she won the 1982 LPGA Championship and the 1983 U.S. Open — seems to surprise people. Stephenson was the first woman to become involved in designing golf courses. Of course, these designing women are the reason for the LPGA's popularity today.

Nancy Lopez is the personality the LPGA likes to promote. She is an attractive, engaging mother who can shoot the lights out on a golf course. By the end of 1986, Lopez had won 34 tournaments. She is part of a well-conceived plan that now offers in excess of eleven million dollars in prizes. The LPGA truly has come a long way, baby.

© Howard O. Allen

In the mid-60s and early-70s, when Kathy Whitworth (left) dominated the LPGA Tour, the prize money offered was small. Since 1977, when Nancy Lopez (right) joined the Tour, the total purses awarded have quadrupled. Over $11 million was won in 1987.

© Jim Moriarty

The Senior PGA Tour

NOW THIS IS A TERRIFIC CONCEPT. LET'S SAY YOU HAVE A GROUP OF athletes past their prime who, nevertheless, can still perform well enough to inspire occasional awe. The sport they play places no tremendous physical demands on their bodies — stealing bases and running back kickoffs through a maze of hurtling opponents is not part of the program — leaving open the possibility of a long and fruitful career. Yet, it's obvious these older gentleman can't compete with the younger fellows. What to do?

You invent the Senior PGA Tour. "Sometimes," says Chi Chi Rodriguez, "I think I've died and gone to heaven."

Small wonder. Since 1980, the Senior Tour has been a boon to players like Rodriguez, who won just over $1 million in twenty years on the PGA Tour. In 1986 and 1987 alone, Rodriguez won more than $800,000 at fifty-two, an age at which some men consider retirement. The growth of the Senior Tour is unprecedented in sports. What began in 1980 with two tournaments and a total purse of $250,000 is now a thirty-five event extravaganza that offers competitors fifty years or older a chance to compete for $8.8 million.

They open the season, just as they used to, in California, and swing through Arizona, Texas, and Florida until the weather is suitable in places like Ohio and Massachusetts. A serviceable senior can win a $45,000 first prize in a large tournament and a minimum of $26,500 for a lesser victory.

By joining the Senior PGA Tour, Arnold Palmer lent the organization credibility— and its popularity grew.

© Bob Daemmrich

Chi Chi Rodriguez (left) *and Billy Casper* (right) *have been two of the top money-winners on the Senior Tour.*

© R. Mackson/FPG Intl.

It began in 1978 with the Liberty Mutual Legends of Golf at Onion Creek Country Club in Austin, Texas. Promoters wondered if golf fans would come out to see some of the great names from that past. The answer was an unqualified yes, and the team tournament, won by Sam Snead and Gardner Dickinson, was a success. They staged it again in 1979, and this time more blasts from the past competed, with Julius Boros and Roberto De Vicenzo taking first prize. In 1980, Tommy Bolt and Art Wall were the reigning legends. That was the year the United States Golf Association began the U.S. Senior Open. The PGA Tour, under the direction of commissioner Deane Beman, added a few more experimental tournaments.

Suddenly, the leaderboards of the 1960s seemed to have been transported into the 1980s. At age forty-seven, Don January had been good enough to win the PGA Tour's Vardon Trophy, symbolic of the circuit's lowest scoring average, in this case a remarkable 70.56. In a matter of six years, January earned more on the Senior Tour than he had in a distinguished 25-year career on the PGA Tour. Through 1986, January had won twenty-five tournaments to become the dominant player in the early stages of the Senior Tour. Another familiar name was Miller Barber. He was the fastest senior to pass the $1-million mark after January, winning nineteen tournaments through 1986. Gene Littler, Australia's Peter Thomson, Lee Elder, and Billy Casper are other

Both Gary Player (left) *and Sam Snead* (below) *capped successful careers by playing on the Senior Tour.*

golfers who have aged gracefully and won the greatest share of the money.

The Senior Tour appeals to golf fans for a number of reasons. First of all, there is a built-in gallery. Anyone who followed Casper in his heyday would quite naturally be interested in rooting for him as he continued on in the game. As golf took hold in the 1950s and 1960s, legions of fans were produced. And now they grow older, along with their favorite stars. The senior's game is also one with which the spectators are familiar. These players do not crush their drives 300 yards off the tee. As the raw power diminishes, accuracy becomes more important, and most of the seniors are deadly with their short irons. Putting, of course, is another thing. As nerve and eyesight begin to fail, scores rise accordingly. This is what really separates the seniors from their younger counterparts on the PGA Tour.

The Senior Tour is also a place for second chances and second careers. Take Jim Ferree, who through 1986 was the Tour's ninth-leading all-time money–winner with $544,167. He tried the PGA Tour in 1956 and won exactly one tournament in eleven years — the Vancouver Centennial, in 1958. His total earnings on the PGA Tour were $107,719, and he eventually became the head professional at Long Cove Club on Hilton Head Island, South Carolina. In 1986, Ferree equaled his PGA Tour total with a victory in the Greater Grand Rapids Open. John Brodie, the former All-Pro quarterback for the San Francisco 49ers, gave up his NBC broadcasting job to try his hand at the Tour.

The man who really made the Senior Tour work, of course, was Arnold Palmer. He lent credibility to the effort, and his dramatic playoff victory over Billy Casper and Bob Stone in the 1981 U.S. Senior Open underlined the competitive nature of these aging atheletes. Palmer's consistent performances proved that charging is something that still can happen after the age of fifty. Gary Player is another legend who has made the successful transition. Soon, a new face will be out on the Senior Tour, matching them divot for divot. In 1990, Jack Nicklaus becomes eligible for the Senior Tour.

Golf Legends Chronology

1400 — Golf is abolished in Scotland by King James II, after his soldiers begin to pass up archery practice in lieu of the sport.

1860 — The inaugural British Open is held. Willie Park wins with a score of 174 over 36 holes, or just under five shots a hole.

1870 — A composite golf ball made of Malaya gutta percha, ground cork, metal filings, and leather replaces a leather pouch stuffed with feathers.

1888 — Golf comes to the United States, arriving at the St. Andrews Club of New York.

1904 — James Braid of England shoots a third-round score of 69 at the British Open, the first sub-70 round in Open history.

1913 — Francis Ouimet, a twenty-year-old amateur from Boston, beats British aces Harry Vardon and Ted Ray in the U.S. Open, putting golf on the map in America.

1922 — Sam Ryder, a British seed merchant, donates a trophy bearing his name for an event which will be contested every two years by teams from America and Great Britain.

1924–27 — Walter Hagen makes a splash by winning four consecutive Professional Golf Association Championship titles, a record that still stands.

1926 — The steel shaft is legalized in the United States, replacing the hickory shaft.

1930 — Bobby Jones wins the Open and Amateur championships of both Great Britain and the United States. His Grand Slam feat is never equaled.

1934 — Paul Runyan's $6,767 in winnings is the leading total in the PGA's inaugural year.

1935 — Gene Sarazen hits one of the most famous shots in golfing history, a double-eagle at the par-five No. 15 hole at Augusta. The final-round stroke of genius helps force a tie at the Masters. Sarazen wins a playoff the next day.

1940 — Bobby Locke perfects the art of putting with his influential overlapping grip.

1943 — Thanks to World War II, the PGA offers only three tournaments with a total purse of $17,000 — the smallest in history.

1944 — Ellen Griffin, Betty Hicks, and Hope Seignious form the Women's Professional Golf Association, the forerunner of the LPGA.

1945 — Byron Nelson wins an incredible 11 consecutive tournaments.

GOLF LEGENDS

1950 — Babe Zaharias wins five of nine tournaments in the LPGA's first season, pocketing $2,875 along the way.

1958 — Arnold Palmer birdies the last three holes at the Masters to beat Ken Venturi by a stroke. It is his first "charge," and the mobilization of Arnie's Army isn't far behind.

1963 — Mickey Wright wins 13 of 32 LPGA tournaments — 40 percent of the year's events.

1963 — Arnold Palmer wins seven tournaments and earns $128,230, becoming the first golfer to reach six figures in winnings.

1965 — At the age of fifty-two, Sam Snead wins the Greensboro Open. It is the last of his PGA-record 84 tournaments wins.

1968 — JoAnne Carner wins a record fifth U.S. Amateur Championship at the age of twenty-nine. She turns professional at thirty.

1970 — Jack Nicklaus becomes golf's first millionaire with a second-place finish in the Bing Crosby Open.

1971 — Captain Alan Shepard of Apollo 14 drills two shots with a telescopic six-iron — on the moon.

1971 — Laura Baugh becomes the youngest woman to win the United States Open. She is sixteen.

1977 — Tom Watson and Jack Nicklaus engage in one of the great duels in golfing history. Both players shoot identical rounds of 68-70-65 at the British Open at Turnberry, but Watson wins on the final day with a 65 — one better than Nicklaus' 66.

1980 — PGA Commissioner Deane Beman creates the Senior PGA Tour.

1980 — Tom Watson wins six tournaments and takes home $530,808.33, becoming the first golfer to crack the half-million dollar mark.

1981 — Kathy Whitworth becomes the first woman golfer to earn $1 million in career winnings.

1982 — Mac O'Grady earns a place on the PGA Tour via Qualifying School — on his seventeenth try. His first attempt was in 1971.

1984 — Kathy Whitworth wins the Rochester International for a career record of 85 tournament victories.

1987 — At the age of thirty, Nancy Lopez is inducted into the LPGA Hall of Fame.

1987 — Jack Nicklaus becomes the first golfer to clear $5 million in career earnings.

United States Open Champions — Men

Year	Name	Year	Name	Year	Name	Year	Name
1901	Willie Anderson	1924	Cyril Walker	1948	Ben Hogan	1968	Lee Trevino
1902	L. Auchterlonie	1925	Willie MacFarlane	1949	Cary Middlecoff	1969	Orville Moody
1903	Willie Anderson	1926	Bobby Jones	1950	Ben Hogan	1970	Tony Jacklin
1904	Willie Anderson	1927	Tommy Armour	1951	Ben Hogan	1971	Lee Trevino
1905	Willie Anderson	1928	John Farrell	1952	Julius Boros	1972	Jack Nicklaus
1906	Alex Smith	1929	Bobby Jones	1953	Ben Hogan	1973	Johnny Miller
1907	Alex Ross	1930	Bobby Jones	1954	Ed Furgol	1974	Hale Irwin
1908	Fred McLeod	1931	Wm. Burke	1955	Jack Fleck	1975	Lou Graham
1909	George Sargent	1932	Gene Sarazen	1956	Cary Middlecoff	1976	Jerry Pate
1910	Alex Smith	1933	John Goodman	1957	Dick Mayer	1977	Hubert Green
1911	John McDermott	1934	Olin Dutra	1958	Tommy Bolt	1978	Andy North
1912	John McDermott	1935	Sam Parks Jr.	1959	Billy Casper	1979	Hale Irwin
1913	Francis Ouimet	1936	Tony Manero	1960	Arnold Palmer	1980	Jack Nicklaus
1914	Walter Hagen	1937	Ralph Guldahl	1961	Gene Littler	1981	David Graham
1915	Jerome Travers	1938	Ralph Guldahl	1962	Jack Nicklaus	1982	Tom Watson
1916	Chick Evans	1939	Byron Nelson	1963	Julius Boros	1983	Larry Nelson
1919	Walter Hagen	1940	Lawson Little	1964	Ken Venturi	1984	Fuzzy Zoeller
1920	Edward Ray	1941	Craig Wood	1965	Gary Player	1985	Andy North
1921	Jim Barnes	1946	Lloyd Mangrum	1966	Billy Casper	1986	Ray Floyd
1922	Gene Sarazen	1947	L. Worsham	1967	Jack Nicklaus	1987	Scott Simpson
1923	Bobby Jones						

Note: The U.S. Open was not played in 1917–18 or 1942–45.

United States Open Champions — Women

Year	Name	Year	Name	Year	Name	Year	Name
1948	Babe Zaharias	1958	Mickey Wright	1968	Susie Maxwell Berning	1978	Hollis Stacy
1949	Louise Suggs	1959	Mickey Wright	1969	Donna Caponi	1979	Jerilyn Britz
1950	Babe Zaharias	1960	Betsy Rawls	1970	Donna Caponi	1980	Amy Alcott
1951	Betsy Rawls	1961	Mickey Wright	1971	JoAnne Carner	1981	Pat Bradley
1952	Louise Suggs	1962	Marie Lindstrom	1972	Susie Maxwell Berning	1982	Janet Alex
1953	Betsy Rawls	1963	Mary Mills	1973	Susie Maxwell Berning	1983	Jan Stephenson
1954	Babe Zaharias	1964	Mickey Wright	1974	Sandra Haynie	1984	Hollis Stacy
1955	Fay Crocker	1965	Carol Mann	1975	Sandra Palmer	1985	Kathy Baker
1956	Mrs. K. Cornelius	1966	Sandra Spuzich	1976	JoAnne Carner	1986	Jane Geddes
1957	Betsy Rawls	1967	Catherine Lacoste	1977	Hollis Stacy	1987	Laura Davies

Masters Tournament Champions

Year	Winner	Year	Winner	Year	Winner	Year	Winner
1934	Horton Smith	1950	Jimmy Demaret	1963	Jack Nicklaus	1976	Ray Floyd
1935	Gene Sarazen	1951	Ben Hogan	1964	Arnold Palmer	1977	Tom Watson
1936	Horton Smith	1952	Sam Snead	1965	Jack Nicklaus	1978	Gary Player
1937	Byron Nelson	1953	Ben Hogan	1966	Jack Nicklaus	1979	Fuzzy Zoeller
1938	Henry Picard	1954	Sam Snead	1967	Gay Brewer Jr.	1980	Severiano Ballesteros
1939	Ralph Guldahl	1955	Cary Middlecoff	1968	Bob Goalby	1981	Tom Watson
1940	Jimmy Demaret	1956	Jack Burke	1969	George Archer	1982	Craig Stadler
1941	Craig Wood	1957	Doug Ford	1970	Billy Casper	1983	Severiano Ballesteros
1942	Byron Nelson	1958	Arnold Palmer	1971	Charles Coody	1984	Ben Crenshaw
1946	Herman Keiser	1959	Art Wall Jr.	1972	Jack Nicklaus	1985	Bernhard Langer
1947	Jimmy Demaret	1960	Arnold Palmer	1973	Tommy Aaron	1986	Jack Nicklaus
1948	Claude Harmon	1961	Gary Player	1974	Gary Player	1987	Larry Mize
1949	Sam Snead	1962	Arnold Palmer	1975	Jack Nicklaus		

Note: The Masters was not played in 1943–45.

PGA Champions

Year	Name	Year	Name	Year	Name	Year	Name
1921	Walter Hagan	1938	Paul Runyan	1956	Jack Burke	1973	Jack Nicklaus
1922	Gene Sarazen	1939	Henry Picard	1957	Lionel Hebert	1974	Lee Trevino
1923	Gene Sarazen	1940	Byron Nelson	1958	Dow Finsterwald	1975	Jack Nicklaus
1924	Walter Hagen	1941	Victor Ghezzi	1959	Bob Rosburg	1976	Dave Stockton
1925	Walter Hagen	1942	Sam Snead	1960	Jay Hebert	1977	Lanny Wadkins
1926	Walter Hagen	1944	Bob Hamilton	1961	Jerry Barber	1978	John Mahaffey
1927	Walter Hagen	1945	Byron Nelson	1962	Gary Player	1979	David Graham
1928	Leo Diegel	1946	Ben Hogan	1963	Jack Nicklaus	1980	Jack Nicklaus
1929	Leo Diegel	1947	Jim Ferrier	1964	Bob Nichols	1981	Larry Nelson
1930	Tommy Armour	1948	Ben Hogan	1965	Dave Marr	1982	Ray Floyd
1931	Tom Creavy	1949	Sam Snead	1966	Al Geiberger	1983	Hal Sutton
1932	Olin Dutra	1950	Chandler Harper	1967	Don January	1984	Lee Trevino
1933	Gene Sarazen	1951	Sam Snead	1968	Julius Boros	1985	Hubert Green
1934	Paul Runyan	1952	James Turnesa	1969	Ray Floyd	1986	Bob Tway
1935	Johnny Revolta	1953	Walter Burkemo	1970	Dave Stockton	1987	Larry Nelson
1936	Denny Shute	1954	Melvin Harbert	1971	Jack Nicklaus		
1937	Denny Shute	1955	Doug Ford	1972	Gary Player		

Leading Money Winners — Men

Year	Name	U.S. Dollars	Year	Name	U.S. Dollars	Year	Name	U.S. Dollars	Year	Name	U.S. Dollars
1934	Paul Runyan	6,767	1949	Sam Snead	31,593	1963	Arnold Palmer	128,230	1977	Tom Watson	310,653
1935	Johnny Revolta	9,543	1950	Sam Snead	35,758	1964	Jack Nicklaus	113,284	1978	Tom Watson	362,429
1936	Horton Smith	7,682	1951	Lloyd Mangrum	26,088	1965	Jack Nicklaus	140,752	1979	Tom Watson	462,636
1937	Harry Cooper	14,139	1952	Julius Boros	37,032	1966	Billy Casper	121,944	1980	Tom Watson	530,808
1938	Sam Snead	19,534	1953	Lew Worsham	34,002	1967	Jack Nicklaus	188,988	1981	Tom Kite	375,699
1939	Henry Picard	10,303	1954	Bob Toski	65,819	1968	Billy Casper	205,168	1982	Craig Stadler	446,462
1940	Ben Hogan	10,655	1955	Julius Boros	65,121	1969	Frank Beard	175,223	1983	Hal Sutton	426,668
1941	Ben Hogan	18,358	1956	Ted Kroll	72,835	1970	Lee Trevino	157,037	1984	Tom Watson	476,260
1942	Ben Hogan	13,143	1957	Dick Mayer	65,835	1971	Jack Nicklaus	244,490	1985	Curtis Strange	542,321
1944	Byron Nelson	37,968	1958	Arnold Palmer	42,407	1972	Jack Nicklaus	320,542	1986	Greg Norman	653,296
1945	Byron Nelson	63,336	1959	Art Wall, Jr.	53,167	1973	Jack Nicklaus	308,362	1987	Curtis Strange	953,296
1946	Ben Hogan	42,556	1960	Arnold Palmer	75,262	1974	Johnny Miller	353,201			
1947	Jimmy Demaret	27,936	1961	Gary Player	64,540	1975	Jack Nicklaus	.323,149			
1948	Ben Hogan	36,812	1962	Arnold Palmer	81,448	1976	Jack Nicklaus	266,438			

Note: Figures for the year 1943 were unavailable.

Leading Money Winners — Women

Year	Name	U.S. Dollars	Year	Name	U.S. Dollars	Year	Name	U.S. Dollars	Year	Name	U.S. Dollars
1948	Babe Zaharias	3,400	1958	Beverly Hanson	12,629	1968	Kathy Whitworth	48,379	1978	Nancy Lopez	189,813
1949	Babe Zaharias	4,650	1959	Betsy Rawls	26,774	1969	Carol Mann	49,152	1979	Nancy Lopez	215,987
1950	Babe Zaharias	14,800	1960	Louise Suggs	16,892	1970	Kathy Whitworth	30,235	1980	Beth Daniel	231,000
1951	Babe Zaharias	15,087	1961	Mickey Wright	22,236	1971	Kathy Whitworth	41,181	1981	Beth Daniel	206,977
1952	Betsy Rawls	14,505	1962	Mickey Wright	21,641	1972	Kathy Whitworth	65,063	1982	JoAnne Carner	310,399
1953	Louise Suggs	19,816	1963	Mickey Wright	31,269	1973	Kathy Whitworth	82,854	1983	JoAnne Carner	291,404
1954	Patty Berg	16,011	1964	Mickey Wright	29,800	1974	JoAnne Carner	87,094	1984	Betsy King	266,771
1955	Patty Berg	16,492	1965	Kathy Whitworth	28,658	1975	Sandra Palmer	94,805	1985	Nancy Lopez	416,472
1956	Marlene Hagge	20,235	1966	Kathy Whitworth	33,517	1976	Judy Rankin	150,734	1986	Pat Bradley	492,021
1957	Patty Berg	16,272	1967	Kathy Whitworth	32,937	1977	Judy Rankin	122,890	1987	Ayako Okamoto	466,034

Index